Van Dusen, Henry Pitney, 1897- ed.
Christianity on the march

CHRISTIANITY ON THE MARCH

Christianity
on the March

HENRY P. VAN DUSEN, *Editor*

CYRIL C. RICHARDSON

WILHELM PAUCK

ROBERT T. HANDY

RAJAH BHUSHANAM MANIKAM

JOHN C. BENNETT

TOM F. DRIVER

HARPER & ROW, PUBLISHERS
NEW YORK, EVANSTON, AND LONDON

To

THE WOMEN'S COMMITTEE

of Union Theological Seminary

and especially to its chairmen

Mrs. Dwight W. Morrow

Mrs. Thomas S. Lamont

Mrs. Frederick A. O. Schwarz

Mrs. Richard S. Perkins

and its Executive Secretary

Mrs. George C. Barclay

Contents

Preface

These chapters were given originally as lectures in the "January Monday Morning Lecture Series" sponsored by the Women's Committee of Union Theological Seminary, New York City.

A decade ago, the Women's Committee, greatly daring, announced a series of four lectures to be given on the Monday mornings of January by members of the Union faculty on theological, spiritual, and practical themes with which they are accustomed to deal in their regular Seminary classes. Interested church women of New York City and its environs were invited to attend. The lecturers were instructed to make no special concessions to the character of their audiences. The lectures were to be a full fifty minutes in length; they were to be delivered in an ordinary classroom setting; they were to be directed to major issues for Christian faith and the church in the life of today. In both form and content, they were to be the sort of presentations which these professors might make to their theological students or to pastors' conferences.

One can recall the uncertainties and misgivings which shadowed so bold and unconventional a project. From the outset, the response far surpassed the most optimistic hopes of the sponsors. At the opening lecture of the first series, the attendance overflowed the Seminary's largest lecture hall and had to be quickly moved to the James Chapel with a seating capacity of 450, where all subsequent lectures have been held. Each January Monday morning through the past decade, from 350 to 450 women of the metropolitan New York area have braved the hazards of January weather and the competition of midwinter holidays in Florida, Bermuda, or the Caribbean to crowd, and sometimes overcrowd, the Chapel.

Each year, there has been insistent demand that the lectures be made available in mimeographed form for leisured study and wider circulation. There have been frequent requests that they be published. This book is a response to that suggestion.

The 1962 series took as its theme "Christianity on the March." Four lectures sought to set forth the pilgrimage of the Christian Movement down the centuries from its earliest outburst upon the Greco-Roman world of the first century to the present; these constitute Parts I and II of the book. It was felt that it would be appropriate as well as useful to complement the historical review with some discussion of the principal alternatives confronting Christian faith in today's world; accordingly, material has been drawn from lecture series of earlier years for Part III.

With minor exceptions, these chapters reproduce the lectures as they were actually spoken. The "existential" character of the original delivery needs to be borne in mind: the limitations of a fifty-minute period; the nature of the audience;

the intimate, sometimes off-the-cuff, immediacy of utterance face-to-face to an alert and eager company of some four hundred laywomen. It is hoped that readers will sense, and welcome, the direct, informal spoken word through the printed page.

We are glad to seize this opportunity to pay tribute to the magnificent group of able and devoted women who have sponsored this project. Under the imaginative and inspired leadership of Mrs. Dwight W. Morrow, the first and at the beginning the only woman Director of Union Theological Seminary, a dozen colleagues joined in 1948 to form a "Women's Committee" to further the life and work of the Seminary, in which they had become keenly interested. They turned their attention and boundless energies, in the first instance, to aspects of the Seminary which most naturally fell within their special concern—the adequacy and beauty of Union's physical plant and the special problems and welfare of three groups within the student body: women who constitute one-fourth of the student community; student wives, numbering over 250; and the nearly one hundred foreign students from some thirty-five countries overseas. The greatly enhanced charm of Union's social facilities and the increased comfort and happiness of these three groups within the larger Seminary community bear grateful testimony to the untiring solicitude and activity of the Women's Committee.

After a few years, however, the members of the Committee expressed the wish that a very much larger number of women of metropolitan New York might receive something of the intellectual stimulus and spiritual enrichment which this association had brought to many of them. Hence, their plan for the Monday Morning Lectures in January. This book is offered as a small tribute to the members of the Women's Committee, its successive chairmen, and its devoted and effective Executive Secretary.

H. P. V. D.

Union Theological Seminary
New York, New York
Easter Day, 1963

PART I

CHRISTIANITY'S MARCH
THROUGH HISTORY

1. The Beginning: Turning the World Upside Down

CYRIL C. RICHARDSON

"Turning the world upside down"—the text from which this topic is suggested is to be found in the *Acts of the Apostles* (17:6). There, in the colorful language of the Authorized Version, "certain lewd fellows of the baser sort" were stirred by disaffected Jews to storm the house of Jason in Thessalonica, where Paul and Silas were staying. Not finding the apostles, the mob hailed Jason and some of the brethren before the city magistrates, charging that they had turned the world upside down and in particular were undermining the empire by claiming, "There is another king, one Jesus." It is this political charge leveled against Christianity that will serve as the first theme of this chapter.

There are many ways in which Christianity upset the world into which it was born. We cannot of course consider them all. We must confine ourselves to three of them. I intend to deal first with the causes of Christian persecution in the Roman empire, for it is here that the conflict between the prevalent culture and the new faith becomes most apparent. Then I shall examine the religious revolution which Christianity set afoot in terms of philosophy and the mystery religions. Finally I shall treat the rise of Christian asceticism— a topic which is all the more important because the monastic movement upset the ancient social structures in no small degree, and Protestants are apt not to give it due attention since the Reformation renounced the principle of dual morality. That, then, is our program: the causes of Christian persecution, Christianity as the new philosophy and mystery religion, and the rise of Christian asceticism.

Before embarking on these themes, however, I want to make two preliminary observations. The first is this: We are likely to imagine that our faith was born into a stable world which it proceeded to revolutionize. While there is an element of truth in this, it is far more correct to look upon the Roman world as itself undergoing a series of revolutions. Christianity was the most notable but not the only one of these. From the murder of Julius Caesar in 44 B.C. to the crowning of Charlemagne in A.D. 800, the Mediterranean world had experienced the most profound changes. To these Christianity contributed in fundamental ways. But the changes were also wrought by other factors. Christianity entered a dynamic world that was being constantly revolutionized. At the very time Christ was born, Augustus was transforming the old republican structures into the new imperium. Within two centuries the empire was plunged into an exhausting period of civil wars, to emerge under the tutelage of Diocletian and Constantine as a highly centralized social system, with a bureaucracy headed by emperors who assumed the pomp and ceremony of the Oriental courts. The capital was transferred to the East, first to Nicomedia, then to

Constantinople. There followed the barbarian invasions which brought the collapse of the West and the foundation of Teutonic kingdoms, at first Arian in their religious affiliation and later Catholic with the rise of the Franks. The whole scene, moreover, was radically altered by the swift succession of military conquests by the new world-religion of Islam, which extended from Persia to the Pyrennees and hemmed in both the Byzantine empire and the Christian West throughout the Middle Ages.

Nor was the world of thought without profound changes through all this period. The crowning achievement of ancient philosophy was to come in the third century with the rise of Neoplatonism, and this itself was radically to inform the Christian religion. The greatest Eastern theologian, Origen, was a pupil of the same master as Plotinus—Ammonius Saccus, perhaps the real founder of Neoplatonism. Equally did aspects of the Teutonic culture of the so-called barbarian invaders affect Christianity, with the result that the medieval faith to which we owe so large a debt was transformed by Teutonic ways of thinking. I mention these things merely to emphasize that the picture should not be one of Christianity upsetting a stable world, but one of Christianity dynamically molding a world in constant change, and itself being affected by these successive revolutions.

My second preliminary observation must be this: The "world" of which we are thinking is a fraction—a bare fraction—of the inhabited globe. It is merely the Mediterranean basin. "Turning the 'world' upside down" means upsetting what its citizens imagined, with a good deal of arrogance compounded with ignorance, was the "civilized" world. The actual word used in our text is *oikoumene*, by which the Greek contrasted *his* world with that of "outsiders." The world which Christianity affected was only a small part of the earth; and we should do well to realize that other civilizations were flourishing, and for centuries remained untouched by the new faith. Even today only about a third of the world's population can be called Christian; and a good deal less than a third of our world can be legitimately considered as deeply influenced by Christian attitudes and beliefs.

With these things in mind, then—that Christianity was born into a world rapidly changing and itself undergoing its own revolutions (quite apart from the new faith) and that the "world" we are speaking of was but a fraction of the earth's population and surface—let us turn to our first theme—the causes of Christian persecution.

CHRIST AND CAESAR

At the moment when Christ the King was born there was emerging the divine kingship of the Roman empire. The first three centuries represent the struggle between the rival claims of Christ and Caesar, a struggle which ends only with the conversion of Constantine and the beginnings of the Byzantine empire. It is the struggle of *kyrios Christos* against *kyrios kaisar*. These terms are highly suggestive. The first is the earliest confession of faith which Paul indicates that Christians made at their baptism (I Cor. 12:3), while the other is the profession of patriotism and loyalty which was demanded of the Roman citizen. The aged Polycarp, the bishop of Smyrna, being taken to his martyrdom was urged by the police captain in these very words: "What harm is it to say *kyrios kaisar* and to offer sacrifice and to save your skin?"[1]

"What harm?" To understand what was here involved we must appreciate the close association which existed in the

Roman mind between religion and patriotism, and the special meaning this had in the rise of the principate under Augustus. After the murder of Julius Caesar, Octavius Augustus rose to power and Caesarism was born. While he kept the outward appearances of the old republic and indeed wanted to go down in history as its restorer, in actual fact the principate which he founded and in which he functioned as "princeps," or first citizen, was altogether different from the old regime. It was an absolutism veiled under the fiction of the old republican forms. It was indeed a necessity for a far-flung empire, whose administration could not be adequately conducted along the old federal and representative lines. But it was more than a political revolution; it was a religious revolution too. Augustus thought of himself as the reviver of the traditional piety and Roman religion; but just as he was in fact an innovator in politics, so the religious aspect of Caesarism begun with him was equally an innovation. The emperor was a sacred person, and the ancient cult of the divinity of kings was a feature of Octavius' religious revival. He tried, indeed, to keep it within bounds. While his "genius" (the guardian spirit, that is, of his *paterfamilias*) was placed in the shrines on the street corners, and while technically the emperor was not divine (*divus*) until his death, after which divine honors were granted the deceased ruler by the Senate in accordance with his worthy rule and miracles attesting his deification (as had happened in the case of Julius Caesar), nonetheless in the popular imagination he was virtually a god, and the claim was pressed by his successors. Caligula could say to the Jewish embassy which waited upon him, "You are the wretches who do not believe I am a god," and Domitian could style himself *"dominus et deus,"* reminding us of Thomas' confession, "My Lord and my God" (John 20:28). The concrete reality of Rome's majesty was expressed in the divine emperor. Nor were the provinces backward in acknowledging this. For them the divinity of kings was an age-long conviction, and the fact that the orderly administration of the principate had saved them from the extortions and ravages of republican proconsuls gave them special reason to hail Caesar as divine. Provinces vied with each other in their festivals in his honor, and loyalty to Caesarism became a test of patriotism. Caesar was king of a world-wide empire of peace (the *pax Romana*); he was the first citizen of a universal brotherhood of free men, to which Caracalla had extended the benefits of Roman citizenship; he was lord and savior who had redeemed the empire from the corruptions of the ancient regime. To fail to honor Caesar was to deny the very foundations of civilized, social life. It was to evidence oneself as a "hater of the human race" (as Tacitus styled the Christian), a despiser of those sanctions by which men could live in peace and brotherhood.

Nor was the demand made that this loyalty should be exclusive. The imperial policy toward religion was one of large toleration. Manifold cults flourished everywhere; even the city of Rome ("That sink," Tacitus says, "into which everything filthy flows.") admitted foreign cults. Isis and *Magna Mater* (Cybele) finally gained entrance into the city, while liberty of speculation was permitted as long as one was patriotic. The syncretic spirit of the age, a consequence largely of the far-flung empire, welcomed a multitude of gods into the Roman Pantheon. To pay one's religious respects to Caesar was not to renounce one's ancestral faith. Rather was it to enlarge it, and to give a religious foundation to one's patriotism.

It is precisely this which the Christian refused. His answer

ΙΧΘΥΣ

was clear-cut and unambiguous. His religious loyalty was
exclusive. It could never be a question of Christ *and* Caesar
in one pantheon. It was always and only a question of Christ
or Caesar. Men are but men—and only once, and only in
Jesus, had God become incarnate and redeemed the world.
The peace and brotherhood of the empire were not grounded
in a divine sanction. They were human institutions, not incarnations of the divine. Civilized life was secondary to
citizenship in heaven. Listen to the court record of the
Christians arraigned before the proconsul Vigellius Saturninus in Scili in North Africa:

SATURNINUS: Swear by the genius of our lord, the emperor.
SPERATUS: The empire of this world I know not.
SATURNINUS: Will you take time to think it over?
SPERATUS: In a matter so straightforward, there is no point in
reconsidering.
SATURNINUS: Have a delay of thirty days.
SPERATUS: I am a Christian.

They are condemned to death. Nartzalus says:

Today we are martyrs in heaven: Thanks be to God.

It was as simple as that; and with that simplicity (Speratus
actually calls it *mysterium simplicitatis*) Christianity turned
the world upside down. The confusion of religion with politics, the assimilation of civilized life to heavenly citizenship
were broken. The transcendence of God and his unique
revelation in Jesus were asserted against the claims that
human life is divine and that the established order and its
representatives are fit objects of worship. The Christian
affirmed a new loyalty and made himself a rebel against a
world that thought of itself as incorporating the divine. The
secular state was born. The divinity of kings was overthrown.

Man freed himself from the false notion that a way of life was itself god. He was willing to suffer for a new conception of human existence, which did not confuse the things to be rendered to Caesar with the things to be rendered to God.

"But what harm is it to say 'Lord Caesar' and to offer sacrifice and save your skin?" So spoke the police officer to Polycarp. And he replied: "I am not going to do what you urge on me." And they gave up the attempt to persuade him. So he was martyred, saying: "For eighty-six years I have been Christ's servant. How can I blaspheme my King?"

PHILOSOPHIES AND THE MYSTERIES

Let us turn now to our second theme and consider Christianity as a revolution in religion. Apart from the question of the imperial cult, the two most significant expressions of religion in the Roman empire were the mystery religions and philosophy. Civic and national cults continued to flourish, but they were of a formal nature. What distinguished the mysteries and philosophy was that they involved personal commitment. In a day which saw a decline of the citizen's direct participation in government with the rise of the imperium, these religions spoke immediately to the human heart. The individual, who seemed to count but little in the scheme of things, found here a meaning for his existence and satisfied the age-old yearnings for cleansing, salvation, and insight into the significance of human life. From these religions Christianity took not a little as it developed its own vocabulary, thought, and customs; and while, as we shall see, it sharply contrasted with them, it also had a close affinity with them. Christians could think of themselves as converts to the True Mystery (as did Clement of Alexandria) and as devotees of the Genuine Philosophy (as did Tatian, who remarked, "I embraced our barbaric philosophy").

Of philosophy as religion I have no time to speak adequately here. I should, however, like to make a couple of observations about it. For one thing, not a few of the most distinguished early Christians came to the new faith by a spiritual journey through various philosophies. I think, for instance, of Justin Martyr and Augustine. Their pilgrimage makes us keenly aware that philosophy was not a dry academic subject, but a practical way of life which offered solutions to the meaning of existence and to the perplexing riddles with which man finds himself confronted whenever he asks, "Why am I here?" Existential philosophy in the modern day has recovered this vital, personal element of ancient philosophy (cf. ch. 7 below).

My second observation is that the systems in vogue during the early Christian centuries were eclectic in character. It is from this confluence of many systems that Christianity derived a good deal of its way of thinking, and in their Apologies the early defenders of the new faith made use of the skeptics' attacks on the old mythologies, of the Stoic concern for the harmony and beauty of the universe, of the Aristotelian ethics, and so forth. Perhaps the greatest debt of Christianity to these systems is one owed to Platonism, with its insight into the spiritual world which lies behind the world of sense. In commenting on his own spiritual pilgrimage from Stoic, Peripatetic, Pythagorean, and Platonist to Christian, Justin Martyr notes how "the perception of incorporeal things quite overwhelmed me and the Platonic theory of ideas added wings to my mind."[2] Similarly Augustine could write in his *Confessions*, "In the Platonists God and his word are everywhere implied."[3] It was through the vision of a world beyond our immediate sense and the material things surrounding us, that the way was made possible for many to embrace the gospel. One must look heavenward in order to hope for and then to find the gift that came from heaven.

The cardinal point wherein Christianity differed from philosophy was in its acknowledgment of the incarnation. To the Greeks and Romans this was foolishness, as Paul says (I Cor. 1:23). This was the Christian revolution in philosophy, the assertion that God had entered human life and died for the sins of the world. The Logos which all men eagerly sought had become flesh in an obscure province of the empire. This word, *Logos,* by which John summarizes the gospel, was a key word in many philosophic systems of that day. Logos was what we might call "ultimate meaning," "the truth of existence," "the ground of the world's being." It was a term of great richness, and the Christian took it over to revolutionize it. No longer was it to point to an abstract conception, a mere "idea" of what the world was all about, or to an immanent principle which was as responsible for evil as for good. Rather was it to express the fullness of God's love in his act in Jesus Christ, and to denote in terms of flesh and blood the character of God and the true destiny of man. To grasp that meaning of Logos was, as Justin Martyr observed, to have opened for one "the gates of light," and to penetrate the true mystery of the spiritual world, which even for the Platonist remained hidden till the "fullness of time."

Christianity was not only *the* philosophy, it was also *the* mystery religion, and to this we must now turn. The spirit of inwardness and the yearning for salvation which were begotten of the centralized empire found expression in the widespread mystery religions. Here the initiate underwent a dramatic ceremony of dying and rising; and, being identified with a savior god, acquired new life and salvation, and was assured of triumph over death itself. How like Christianity all this sounds, and how easily could Christianity be interpreted in the very phrases of these ancient cults!

Basically the mystery religions were founded on the ancient fertility myth of dying and rising, which goes back to neolithic times. The story was told in a hundred different ways, but always the basic theme is the same: a savior god conquers death as the course of nature itself passes from life to death and to new life. In Egypt it is Osiris who is slain by his wicked brother Typhon, his body cut into pieces and cast into the river. But the loving and patient spouse Isis recovers his members and so restores him to life. This is the story of the sowing of wheat on the mud flats of the Nile and the resurrection of nature in the annual harvest. In Greece it is the maiden (Kore) Persephone who is carried off to the underworld by the god of wealth, Pluto. In her grief the mother Demeter searches for her and refuses to let the wheat grow. Zeus finally prevails upon Pluto to allow Persephone to spend eight months of the year in the upper world. The descent of Kore is the putting of the grain in the underground silos, and the ascent of the maiden is the opening of the silos and the bringing up of the seed for a new sowing. The "Corn maiden" is thus reunited with the "Corn mother," the old crop being the basis for the new. In Mithraism the connection of agricultural fertility with the slaying of the cosmic bull is not altogether clear, but the same myth of renewal doubtless underlies that religion. The seed of life is in the dying bull, and by its blood the wheat comes to life.

It was this experience of dying and rising that the devotee underwent in his initiation. He became identified with the god who had triumphed over the dark powers of death; and by the rising of the god he was guaranteed a future life. One of the Church Fathers, Firmicus Maternus, describes for us the initiation into the cult of Attis. The image of the god is laid prone on a bed. There is total darkness while the devotees lament the god's tragic fate. Then the priest brings light, smears the throats of the worshipers with oil, and calls out: "Be of good cheer, initiates, the god is safe and sound. And for you too there shall be salvation from all your troubles."

There can be no question that Christianity had a close affinity with these cults and quite properly could be spoken of as a mystery religion. Its dominant theme was the passage from death to life. Burial and resurrection were central in the baptismal rite. Like the mysteries, too, it had its annual festival of resurrection in Easter. Like them its liturgy was presented as a dramatic mystery in which death was conquered. Like them its community was secret, and the initiate was not allowed to divulge the sacramental ceremonies to unbelievers (the *disciplina arcani*). Like them it appealed to religious emotion, had fraternity benefits for its members, and bound them together in a close-knit society. Finally its whole scheme of salvation could most easily be put into the very phrases of the mystery religions. This, indeed, is precisely what Clement of Alexandria did in his *Protreptikos*,[4] an urgent appeal to conversion, addressed to the heathen: "O truly sacred mysteries! O pure light! In the blaze of the torches I have a vision of heaven and of God. I become holy by initiation. The Lord reveals the mysteries. He marks the worshiper with his seal, gives light to guide his way. . . . These are the revels of my mysteries!"

But Christianity also turned the mystery religions upside down, as it revolutionized philosophy. The fundamental question to ask in this regard concerns the way in which the god faces death. Why and with what attitude does the god die? That is the cardinal point. Does he die as did the victims of the pagan mysteries, smitten by the blind forces of fate—dying unwillingly and escaping from the tyranny of an alien world? No. The Christian story is basically, radically different. The Christ dies willingly, submitting to the obedience of the cross to do his Father's will. God takes to himself the sufferings of mankind and in his abounding love transforms them and redeems his fallen creation. It is not to elude the world but to redeem it that this death intervenes. Resurrection is not escape from the endless tale of nature's passage from life to death. No. It is the new act of God by which the world is won to his love, and the abundant mercy of his condescension toward mankind is made manifest. God himself suffers for the sake of man—and he does this willingly, out of pure love, not because he finds escape from a blind necessity that rules over his own nature. This is the Christian revolution of the mystery religions: that God in his freedom stoops down to redeem us, and will even die to make known his love, and to fulfill the purposes of his creation.

Moreover, the story is that of a historic person, not a personification of nature's fertility. This man who lived in Galilee and died in Jerusalem under Pontius Pilate—this man who has a date in the world's history; who is flesh and blood; who shares our nature, our temptations, and our sorrows; who passes through the valley of our death—this one, it is, who dies and rises and brings us new life. We look not to a myth but to facts; not to an idealization of nature's course but to a real human being, in whom God was active, in whom the mystery of God's presence was revealed and the anxiety of death overcome, because God took it to himself and abolished its sting. We are devotees not of a fairy story but of an act of God, proclaimed and made public for all to know in the province of Judea in the first century. It is to those facts of history that the apostles bear witness, and it is that truth which the Gospels and the creeds of the church enshrine.

There were, also, other differences between Christianity and the pagan mysteries. For one thing, Christianity was a society open to the poor and the dispossessed, whereas the costs of initiation into the cults were for the most part high and their membership was limited to higher-income groups. Then too, there was a strong intellectual element in Christianity, lacking in the mysteries. Aristotle's observation that "it is not necessary for the initiate to learn anything, but to receive certain impressions and to be put in a certain frame of mind" was on the whole true of the mysteries. But Christianity developed also as a philosophy. The intellect was not despised; rather was it brought into the service of the faith. Again, the ethical element was more central in Christianity. It was not merely the conquest of death, but the conquest of moral evil, that was central to the gospel. The good news was not only that death was overcome, but that the possibility of a new life of service and fellowship was opened up and demanded here and now. The new faith was very definitely a way of life which called for great sacrifice and stern discipline. One is perpetually struck by how much it cost in terms of one's security to become a Christian in those early days. It was far from easy. Not only was there the danger of persecution, even martyrdom, by refusal to observe the imperial cult, but the Christian had to forgo all manner of trades and virtually revolutionize his life before he could be granted baptism. Listen to the rules in one of the earliest church orders from Rome, about A.D. 197: "If a man is a

pander, . . . if a man is a sculptor, a painter, . . . if a man is an
actor, . . . if a man teach children worldly knowledge, . . .
a charioteer, . . . a gladiator, . . . a soldier, . . . a military
governor, . . . a magician, . . . a charmer, an astrologer, a
man with a concubine, . . . either let him desist or let him
be rejected." All trades involving idolatry, such as the arts,
the theater, education, all trades involving executions such as
military service and the magistracy were forbidden. The
church as a vast friendly society had to find these people new
jobs and turn *them* (as it were) upside down, before they
could be admitted. Christianity involved an ethical and disciplined life consonant with the gospel. It was not so to anything like the same extent in the mysteries, though in a few
cases their moral demands were relatively high.

There was one other notable difference we may mention.
The Christian mystery was exclusive in its loyalty, the cults
were syncretic. Persons sufficiently well-off frequently had
themselves initiated into several mysteries, as a sort of extra
insurance for the world to come. In Christianity it was entirely different. There were not many gods, but one God.
There were not many saviors, but one Savior. To the pagan
the Christian attitude was arrogant and curiously self-assured.
To the Christian the pagan failed to take religion seriously.
One had to be committed—and to be committed inevitably
involves an exclusive attitude. If the way of life in Jesus was
to be embraced, this meant a life of service and love which
absolutely excluded other ways of life. To be sure, not all the
implications of Christianity were early seen. The terrible
custom of slavery, while alleviated by Christianity, was not
abolished; nor were the full implications of the new faith
for social and political life thought through. The early Christian fought on many fronts, but he could not fight on all;

and many of these issues remain with us, unsolved until today. What the early Christian did see with remarkable clarity
was that the demands of the gospel involved exclusiveness.
There could be no traffic between Christ and Isis, between
the Lord God and Zeus. One had to choose and to decide.
Either one cast in one's lot with the fellowship of believers
and acknowledged that God was the God revealed in Jesus,
and undertook that discipline of life, or one could afford to
have many religions and many codes of ethics for different
occasions.

What made the matter so clear-cut in the Christian imagination was the figure of Jesus. The counsels of the Sermon on
the Mount, and the pattern of life he himself had displayed
placed him in an entirely different category from others. If
one embraced that life and acknowledged it as of God, the
decision was made, and no other course could be considered.
Christians thought of themselves as the "new race" of men,
who had penetrated the mystery by which genuine human
life could be lived and the real meaning of existence could
be grasped.

They love one another, and from widows they turn not away
their esteem. They deliver the orphan from him who treats him
harshly. And he who has gives to him who has not, without boast-
ing. And when they see a stranger they take him into their homes
and rejoice over him as a very brother; . . . and whenever one of
their poor passes from the world, each one of them according
to his ability gives heed to him and carefully sees to his burial.
And if they hear that one of their number is imprisoned or
afflicted on account of the name of their Messiah, all of them
anxiously minister to his necessity, and if it is possible to redeem
him they set him free. And if there is among them any that is

poor and needy, and if they have no spare food, they fast two
or three days in order to supply to the needy their lack of food.[5]

Such are the words of Aristides in the second century. The
picture he paints may be somewhat idyllic, but it is not on
that account to be ignored altogether. Not all Christians lived
like that, but undoubtedly a great many did. It was to embrace that kind of life that they gave up worldly security
and often faced martyrdom. That is why they were exclusive
in their loyalty. They believed they had found the meaning
of human existence.

THE ASCETIC LIFE

We pass now to the third and final theme of this chapter.
We must consider the way in which early Christian asceticism
played its part in turning the world upside down. I have
purposely chosen to include this topic not only because of
its historic significance in the early church's mission, but
because it is one which Protestants tend to neglect. The
protests against the monastic life in the sixteenth century
have sometimes led us to underestimate the ascetic role in
Christianity.

From the very beginning of the gospel its demands were
seen to involve a break with some of the normal relationships
of life. But a certain ambiguity here enters in. On the one
hand, Jesus renounces some ascetic elements in John the
Baptist's mission. Jesus' disciples do not fast like the Baptist's
(Mark 2:18 ff.), and in contrast to that desert preacher, Jesus
is known as a "glutton and a winebibber" (Matt. 11:19).
Yet, on the other hand, the gospel in some circumstances does
demand a denial of family relations (Mark 3:35), of posses-

sions (Mark 10:21), and a requirement of poverty for the apostolic mission (Mark 6:7 ff.). While Jesus' preaching of the Kingdom does involve a rejoicing in contrast to the more gloomy message of John, nonetheless the fact that Jesus himself remained unmarried and urged on his disciples a mission of self-denial early led the church to adopt ascetic ways. Fasting becomes a characteristic of the primitive Christian community, and sayings such as there are eunuchs for the Kingdom of Heaven's sake (Matt. 19:12) deeply affected the Christian imagination. A conception of a way of life more "perfect" than that of normal family relations quickly develops, while the renunciation of possessions plays its role in the early Jerusalem community.

Particularly is it in sexual relations that the ascetic temper becomes evident. For Paul the highest type of Christian life is the celibate one ("It is good for a man not to touch a woman," I Cor. 7:1), and he advocates this way of life, which he himself adopts, as his "counsel," though not laying it down as a general law (I Cor. 7:25). One reason for his attitude is that the "time is short" (7:29), and hence with the end immediately in view the Christian has other concerns than that of settling down in a stable world. Moreover, Paul sees marriage and children as an encumbrance. The celibate can care better for the things of the Lord when he is no longer under the obligation of pleasing his wife (I Cor. 7:32-3) and looking after a family. The rapid expansion of Christianity in the Roman world has not a little to do with the fact that the early Christian missionary was an ascetic, and without the duties of family life could the more easily move from place to place, founding churches and spreading the gospel. It was not long, indeed, before some Christians imagined that the ascetic life was the one to which all believers were called, and in the second century we find a bishop of Corinth rebuking a neighboring bishop of Cnossos, in Crete, for putting the brethren under "a heavy, compulsory burden of chastity." Again, at the Council of Nicea in A.D. 325, a movement arose to demand of all clergy that they should be celibate, though through the urging of Paphnutius, a bishop in Upper Thebais, this was finally overruled. The principle, however, ultimately triumphed in the West and in a more limited way in the East where the episcopate became recruited from the monasteries.

Christian asceticism has both a pagan and a Jewish background. Buddhism, of course, for five hundred years before Christ, had developed the monastic life, while recluses of one kind or another were to be found in many religions, notably in the cult of Serapis in Egypt. Moreover, two trends in Greek philosophy played their role in the development of Christian monachism. There was, on the one hand, the Stoic conception of apathy, whereby the wise man so curbed his passions that he was free to live a life of self-containment and reason. On the other hand, there was the Cynic ideal, begun in Diogenes and finding a remarkable revival in the first century, whereby a life of simplicity and freedom from convention and normal obligation was upheld as man's true destiny. The entanglements of society with its disorders and unreality were viewed as opposed to the discovery and development of the true self, which could only flourish and be enlarged in isolation and in retirement from the world.

Nor were the Jews without a similar inclination to asceticism. The recent discovery of the Qumran scrolls has cast a flood of light on sectarian Judaism, and the Dead Sea communities along with those of Damascus and the Therapeutae in Egypt show us a monachism developing from the Hasidim of the Maccabean period. While their attitudes toward marriage and other features of the ascetic life were far from uniform, these communities were distinguished by their withdrawal from the main stream of Jewish life. In retirement they lived either (as in Egypt) cultivating a strict ascetic piety or (on the wastelands near the Dead Sea) in communities under a disciplined way of life, awaiting the appearance of Messiahs who would lead them in triumph in a holy war which would gain for Israel her final destiny.

All these streams played a part in the framing of Christian monachism which was both to affect the spirituality of the church and to inform the Christian culture which emerged from the triumph of the new faith within the empire.

Two types of monasticism arose in the third and fourth centuries and have been perpetuated ever since. One was that of the Egyptian ascetic, Antony, who was the first to give some organized shape to the eremitical life. Here the ideal was that of the solitary hero, who in the loneliness of the desert fought temptation, acquired spiritual self-sufficiency, and extinguished all natural desire. It was a lay and individualistic movement, a protest at once against the evils of society and the secularization of the church. In the place of social and catholic solidarity stood the ideal of the heroic layman who had left all for the sake of Christ, and devoted himself to spiritual warfare with the powers of evil and without interruption from the unreality and conventions of a decaying world.

While this heroic fortitude of the hermit has been an ideal of all monasticism (even Benedict of Nursia assumes it as the highest type), its obvious defects early led to the founding of cenobitic monasticism, where the sense of religious community displaced the emphasis on the heroic individual. The founder of this type of monachism was Pachomias, in Upper

Egypt, and its greatest exponent in the West was Benedict of Nursia (6th century). Daily hours of prayer together, a fixed routine of work, and a moderate rule of life were its marks. In the place of excessive austerities such as were practiced by the extreme Syrian ascetics like Simeon Stylites, emphasis was put upon productive work, and Pachomian and Benedictine monasteries soon became busy, self-supporting communities. Indeed Benedict's concern was that the monastery was to give rather than to receive alms, and all poor law and charity up to the Reformation were in fact regulated by the monastery. A sense of social responsibility displaced the earlier flight from society.

The triumph of cenobitic monachism was of peculiar importance. Here was formed the ideal of true Christian community, and it is to the credit of the monasteries finally to have brought to birth the conception of Christian democracy, which was to influence the government both of church and of state. Though in origin the monastery was autocratically governed by its superior, it gradually developed a more democratic organization under the impetus of its conception of Christian community. At its best the monastery gave the opportunity to foster a way of life which represented the ideal Christian society, sufficiently withdrawn from the obligations of the world to work out the ascetic principles of the gospel, and unimpeded by the conventions of a society only half Christian. To be sure, this was the ideal, and the average monastery fell far short of it. Yet its very existence was a constant challenge to secularized Christianity; and it is from the monastery that increased spirituality again and again flowed into the church to revive and reform it.

It was from the monastery, moreover, that the great missionary ventures were undertaken by which the pagan and barbarian invader was won for Christ. Here Celtic monachism (as well as Benedictine) played a dominant role. More rigorous in his asceticism than his Benedictine brother, distinguished also by an undisciplined restlessness and a mystic vision, the Celtic monk carried the gospel far and wide. From Iona to Lindisfarne, from Luxeuil to Bobbio he went, planting monasteries, organizing churches, and preserving learning in the Dark Ages. These Celtic monks were mystic travelers who tried to imitate the apostolic mission with complete devotion. In an Anglo-Saxon chronicle we observe this sentence so typical of the Celtic vision. It tells of three monks "who stole away from Ireland in a boat without any oars, because they would live in a state of pilgrimage for the love of God, they recked not where." This Celtic monasticism finally gave way to the Roman obedience (notably at the Synod of Whitby in A.D. 663), but its spirit long survived. It informed the British monastery which sent forth such notable missionaries as Boniface, the martyr of the Frisian church.

From the Celtic monastery, too, came the Penitentials, which were to be adapted to the life of the secular church and to provide those rules of conduct and religious direction in the confessional by which the barbarian was educated in Christian living. While we may view such Penitentials as unduly formal and naïve, we must never forget that it was by them that the invader was brought to some measure of disciplined life and to some vision of personal sanctity. The chaos spread by the pagan invader was finally overcome; and the emergence of Christian Europe was not a little due to the fact that the church acted as the educator of the barbarian, adapting its methods to suit the times. It was from the monastery that many of these methods came, as it was from the monastery that the great missionaries, Benedictine as well as Celtic, were recruited.

CONCLUSION

We have surveyed some ways in which early Christianity turned the world upside down. We have glanced at the struggle between Christ and Caesar, and have noted the uncompromising attitude of the Christian who refused to grant divine honors to the state. We have seen how Christianity revolutionized both philosophy and the mystery religions by affirming the significance of the incarnation and that the overcoming of death was wrought in Jesus Christ, a real, historical person and not a personification of the powers of fertility. Finally we have looked at the ascetic movement in the early church and noted how much it contributed to a heightened sense of spirituality and to the missionizing of the pagan invader. In many other ways Christianity turned the world upside down, and of all of them we are the heirs. May God grant us the same singleminded devotion as the early martyr, the same sure conviction of His act in Jesus Christ as the early convert to the Christian mystery, and the same spirit of self-denial and missionary fervor as the early Celt.

2. The Great Crisis: The Reformation of the Sixteenth Century

WILHELM PAUCK

Medieval European culture was dominated and shaped by the church, which occupied the center of the common life. Its peculiar dignity and power consisted of two factors. In the first place, men believed it to exhibit the supernatural reality of the divine, the source from which all human existence comes and the end toward which it is directed. As manifested primarily in the priesthood and the sacraments they regarded it as the Body of Christ. This meant that as the people submitted in worship and in daily life to the ministrations of the clergy, they were brought in contact with the reality of Christ, the Incarnate God. Thus the church was believed to transfigure all human existence: The supernatural penetrated the natural; the divine enveloped the human; and eternity absorbed time.

In the second place, the church was the historical mediator which transmitted the cultural legacy of antiquity to the people of Europe. It was the teacher of the new nations of Germanic and Celtic-Romanic origin. Being itself the product of Greco-Roman civilization, particularly in respect of polity and dogma, it transferred to them not only Christianity but also many of the achievements and values which had been produced in antiquity by the Greeks, the Romans, and the Hebrews. Thus the church helped to foster among the new European nations a civilization which was at the same time new and old. It caused the fresh unspent spirit of the European peoples to absorb the accomplishments of the Greeks in philosophy and science, of the Romans in political economy, of the Hebrews in morality and religion. Thus it was through the instrumentality of this institution in which God's eternal plan for salvation was thought to be exhibited that there came into being a *new* civilization, that cultural life which we call Western.

Nothing is more remarkable in all this than the fact that those who felt themselves to be called to forsake the common life and retreat from the world in order to dedicate themselves completely to the pursuit of religion, namely the monks, living in their cloisters, remote from other men, assumed the role of cultural educators and teachers. These unworldly, otherworldly, holy men directed the worldly and profane affairs. All this came to be expressed in the remarkable, largely indigenous institutions of the Middle Ages, its ecclesiasticism and monasticism, but also in its feudal orders and customs.

Now as we approach the topic we are to discuss in this chapter, we must see that, beginning with the fourteenth century, everything in this way of life came to be upset. A period of transition began which was full of crises. The older institutions were shaken up; men's confidence in them became uncertain; a sense of insecurity spread throughout the common life.

For centuries, the Papacy and the Holy Roman empire had been the great universal forces toward which all people oriented themselves. Now the Holy Roman emperors, the leaders of Christendom in the political realm, ceased to be universal rulers. Instead they became dynastic princes pursuing policies of agrandizement directed toward an increase of national or territorial power. And the popes as the bishops of Rome permitted themselves to be preoccupied chiefly with the affairs of their own Italian state, the Patrimony of Peter. They were more concerned for the maintenance of their political power and prestige in the center of Italy than for their responsibility as the rectors and rulers of the church.

These changes were the effect of a great variety of forces. The European peoples were about to mature politically. Nationally unified states were in process of formation in Spain, France, and England. Territorial political units of great diversity were being formed which competed with one another and thus injected a deep restlessness into the common life. Furthermore, the traditional rural barter-economy was gradually being replaced by a money-economy. For the pursuit of this new economic way there developed new social bodies: the towns, centers of a rapidly growing industrialism and commercialism. Both of these produced capitalism, a new economic order which was pointed, on the one hand, to a greater production and distribution of goods and, on the other hand, to the acquisition of profit and the attainment of power over the world through profit.

Moreover, a change came about in the way men looked upon themselves and their earthly scene of action. The fifteenth century was the age of the Great Discoveries. People now learned that what they were accustomed to call the "world," which was actually only the promontory of southern, central, and northern Europe, was but one part of the globe. Their imagination and their sense of the world were incredibly widened when Columbus, the "wonder man" of the era, discovered America and when Vasco da Gama found the seaway around the Cape of Good Hope at the southern tip of Africa.

Under the impact of all these influences, the church necessarily underwent changes. Those who depended upon its services looked at it with new eyes. Its leaders tried to make adjustments to the new conditions. Many of its practices of administration, particularly in connection with appointments and property management, but also in connection with the sacraments, were adapted to the requirements of the new money-economy. As we realize now, the popes who ordered and effected these transformations took tremendous chances, insofar mainly as they used religious ministrations as means of financial transactions; thus they externalized religion. They made their subjects' yearning for salvation a means for economic ends and thus they injected corruptive forces into the body of the church.

The leaders also found methods of aligning the church with the new political forces. The national churches which now developed were formed on the initiative of the secular rulers with the sanction of the popes. Thus these and the territorial churches came more and more under the sway of the political rulers. Many of these rulers intended to be dedicated Christian men, but most of them exploited the church, perhaps unavoidably, for their own political advantage.

Finally this fact has to be noted: Town people became much more independent than their predecessors had been in the old feudal society. Their new way of life rendered them eager and willing for changes of many sorts. Hence they did not hesitate to take the affairs of life in their own hands. The laity began to concern themselves actively with the affairs of the church and brought about a great diversification in the customs and practices of religion.

So it was not surprising that many called for a reform of life and manners, especially in the church. St. Francis and his followers aimed at the imitation of Christ by way of the observance of apostolic poverty. The church, so they taught, must be willing to become poor, and all churchmen must try to achieve spiritual freedom by observing the same utter poverty which characterized the apostles. Others, like Wycliffe and Hus, held that the church should be returned to the order of the Bible. Still others demanded that first the Papacy should be reformed and that its rule over Christendom should be replaced by that of councils and representative assemblies. Many of the monks affirmed that if only all who lived in cloisters would comply with the strictness of the original monastic rules, not only the religious but also the secular life would inevitably be renewed. Thus a great yearning for the renewal came to course through the activities of the church.

Many people, deeply dedicated to the ideals of their own civilization, gave themselves devoutly to the pursuit of religion, confident that ultimately this would bring forth fruit and open up sources of refreshment. Others felt that the end of the world was near; they became engrossed with meditations on death and the world to come or looked for the return of Christ. Still others cultivated the new resources that were available in scholarship, philosophy, literature, and science. They hoped for a renewal of life through education and learning. The humanists, for instance, who had achieved a new sense of human dignity and personal enterprise in connection with their rediscovery of the spirit of Greek and Roman antiquity, encouraged a concern for humanity that was free from arbitrary authoritarian sanctions and animated by the same respect for human creativity which they felt pervaded the works of the ancients. Thus they looked forward to a new cultural life, inspired by the work of scholars, that is, those who had a sense of literature and the art of expression and all the creative faculties of the human mind.

Some, like Ulrich von Hutten, observing how the old gradually fell away and the new emerged to form itself, exclaimed, "It is a joy to be alive!" Others, like Wolfgang Capito, sensing that changes were in the making, remarked, "As far as religion is concerned, there are just two possibilities before us: Either the whole world becomes Christian or all that Christ represents is made irrelevant. There is no other choice."

This was the historical setting in which the Protestant Reformation arose and developed.

However, this statement must not be understood as if it implied the assertion that the Reformation began and took shape by way of a direct continuity with the several movements and undertakings which we have been describing. It is sometimes said that Luther provided the spark which released forces that had been in the making for a long time. One intends to suggest by this that the times were ripe for the emergence of such a movement as the Reformation. But all one should be permitted to say is this: At the beginning of the sixteenth century the human situation in Roman Catholic Europe was so filled with a sense of crisis and an air of expectancy that a leader of the stature of Martin Luther could win wide support because people saw in him the one who seemed able to overcome the crisis by initiating and carrying through a constructive program of action. But saying this does not mean that the European world had been waiting for Martin Luther or that what he stood for had been long in preparation. On the contrary, nobody was more astonished at the fact that he was propelled into the leadership of the movement which became the Protestant Reformation than Martin Luther.

Moreover, what he actually was and represented came as something utterly unexpected to his contemporaries. Those among them who were waiting for the reformation of the church or were actively connected with specific reform-movements certainly did not regard him as the one who fulfilled their historical expectation. The hostile attitude of Erasmus toward Luther exemplifies this in dramatic fashion. Conversely, Luther's almost complete lack of enthusiasm for Erasmus' person and program demonstrates that he did not consider himself or his theological views to be in continuity with what Erasmus symbolized.

And now it is exceedingly fascinating to consider how Luther came to occupy the center of the stage.

It is remarkable that he did not come to the fore in a well-known or important place. Wittenberg, his scene of action, was an insignificant little town on the eastern frontier of the Holy Roman empire, outside the main channels of the cultural life.

What this meant at the time is well illustrated by the following story: After Luther had been banned and when the establishment of reformed churches was in full swing, some of the leaders of each camp, that of the evangelicals as well as that of the Roman Church, looked toward the possibility of a reconciliation. An occasion for one of the first attempts in this direction was afforded in 1530 at the diet of Augsburg in connection with the presentation of the Augsburg Confession, the first creed of the Reformation. Luther's colleague and friend, Philip Melanchthon, professor in the University of Wittenberg, served as the theological spokesman of the Lutherans. He negotiated, in a very responsible but anxious manner, with the representatives of the Roman Church. On one occasion, he was received in audience by one of the eminent prelates of Germany, the Prince-Bishop of Salzburg. This gentleman inquired of Melanchthon why the Lutherans were so insistent on maintaining their own interpretation of Christianity. In his reply, Melanchthon made a reference to conscience. On hearing this, His Grace exclaimed: "Huh, conscience! What is conscience?" Then he suggested that the concerns of the Reformers and of the Roman Catholics could be reconciled. The Roman Church, he said, would make concessions with respect to the marriage of priests, the administration of the Mass, and also in relation to episcopal power, and so on. But, he said, and this is the point of the story, the fact that a bailiwick, namely Wittenberg, should want to bring about a reform of the whole empire constituted, in his opinion, an intolerable disturbance of the public peace! As the occupant of the ancient see of Salzburg he regarded himself as one of the representatives of the well-established Christian civilization; anything coming from Wittenberg impressed him as the product of mere outsiders. Yet the Reformation did arise and spread from there.

Equally important is the fact that its spiritual substance was formed in the unworldliness of a remote cloister. At the time, Luther himself was a faithful Roman Catholic. Against the wishes of his father, he had left the world and become a monk, looking for peace of mind. In a certain way, his father was identified with the new forces of the common life. He had left the homestead of his peasant forebears and had found work as a copper miner. In the course of time, he became quite successful as part-owner of a mine and as a respected member of the community of Mansfeld in which he lived. Recognizing that his son, Martin, was unusually gifted, he saw to it that the child received a good education. He hoped that in due time his son would become a lawyer and as such enjoy an important career as a person of status and influence. And then the boy disappointed him when suddenly, without notifying his parent, he decided to enter a monastery because, he said, he felt that he had "to get a merciful God," that is to say, to make his peace personally with God.

Once in the cloister, Luther endeavored with all his spiritual and moral powers to fulfill the highest of the Biblical commandments, "Thou shalt love the Lord thy God with all thy heart, and with all they soul, and with all thy strength and with all thy mind; and thy neighbor as thyself." While he learned the monastic discipline, he took up the study of theology, on orders of his superiors. He made rapid progress as a student and in due season was appointed a professor of Biblical theology in the new and as yet quite unimportant University of Wittenberg. All the while he underwent the unsettling experience of discovering gradually that the traditional practices and teachings of religion were unable to give satisfaction to him in the deepest searchings of his soul for peace with God. So he was thrown into a struggle for salvation. In the course of it, always in the solitariness of his cell, and as, binding his conscience with absolute honesty to God's word, he tested his faith, he rediscovered the gospel as it spoke to him from the Bible and particularly the writings of

Paul and most especially the Epistle to the Romans. Thus he finally found peace for his soul and, at the same time, answers to his intellectual theological questions.

All the while, he never had the sense that he had found or accomplished something new, but rather, that he had reached the goal he had been pursuing. He had come to understand Christianity, he felt, as a religion of salvation. Before God, he concluded, all men are unworthy insofar as, relying on their own powers, they are never able to fulfill what the Author of everything good expects of them. But because of Christ, so he now thought, men can be sure that, knowing themselves as unworthy in the sight of God, they are nevertheless accepted by him because God's goodness is different from any other kind of goodness. It is mercy, that is, merciful goodness, which through its holiness is able to love even that which is unholy, and thus transforms it. This revelation of divine grace, so Luther now came to see, was the true meaning of the cross of Christ. Hence, he liked to characterize his own exposition of the gospel as the "theology of the cross." Thus he made fresh sense of the very burden of the teaching of Jesus as it is exhibited in the parable of the prodigal son and in such a saying as this: "There is more joy in heaven over one sinner who repents than over ninety-nine who are righteous," that is, who think they are righteous.

As Luther transmitted this understanding, which he cherished as a personal discovery, to his students who were mostly monks like himself, he sensed that there was power in it. But for a long time he did not know of what nature that power was. Then, in 1517, he was drawn into a turmoil which within a few months developed into a movement that concerned the whole Roman Church and upset everything in it. Luther *stumbled* into the Reformation. In a way that was utterly unplanned and unpremeditated, he found himself almost suddenly to be the head of a reforming movement.

It all began when he attacked the sale of indulgences, the undertaking (which was strange, indeed) of selling for money freedom from punishment for sins. He spoke up against this misconception of repentance, hoping for an academic discussion on the power of indulgences which, he thought, might have a beneficial effect upon the teaching of the church. The unexpected result of his protest was that many priests and monks, and also numerous lay people and especially the humanists among them, felt that he was the voice they had been longing to hear for many years. The defenders of the Roman Church, by contrast, hastily accused him of heresy. They were aroused to fury because they suspected that he was directing his attack upon the authority of the Papacy and therefore upon the very foundation of the church.

In defending himself against these critics, Luther relied upon his fresh understanding of the gospel. He was very sure that what he had come to understand was correct. Indeed he felt that the Holy Spirit was on his side insofar, namely, as he knew himself upheld by the primary source and standard of the Christian religion, the Bible. When his opponents suggested to him that he was defying the Papacy, thereby revolting against the ultimate norm of truth in the Christian Church, he had no choice but to pit the authority of the Bible against the authority of the Papacy. At first, he himself did not realize that when he had reached this point he was propelled outside the orbit of the Roman Church and its scholastic teachings.

From now on, he became the spokesman of what he called the "Word of God"—an "evangelist" of God as he had dis-

95 THESES – CASTLE DOOR, WITTENBERG

DIET AT WORMS

closed and kept revealing his nature and will in the Bible over against the papal Antichrist and the unevangelical authority of the Roman Church. Gradually but unavoidably he found himself compelled to launch a program for the reform of the church.

It was several years after he had become prominent as the critic of indulgences and the traditional administration of penance that he acquainted himself closely with the various forms of cultural criticism and the different proposals for reform that had been current for a long time. Then only did he become in a real sense a contemporary of his own era. He found an increasing number of followers everywhere. When he was definitively ordered to change his teachings and to conform to the Roman Church and its traditions, he refused to recant his views, with the result that he was banished first from the church and then from society. Church and empire declared him an outcast.

When as an old man Luther looked back upon the beginning of his career as a reformer, he said, "God led me on as if I were a horse with blinkers on, so that I could not see who came running up against me. A good deed rarely issues from scheming wisdom and resourcefulness. All must happen in the vagaries of ignorance." As the leading reformer, whose destiny it was to interpret the gospel to the Germans as their "prophet," he embodied the utterly unexpected, in the sense that none of those who had looked forward to the rise of a reformer had predicted a leader of the kind he, Luther, actually turned out to be. This is the way in which the great changes in the lives of men almost always occur. They take place when and where no one suspects that they will happen.

And now a brief word about the spread of the Reformation. The instruments which Luther and his followers employed for this purpose were chiefly three: In the first place, preaching; in the second place, pamphlets, the publication and distribution of which represented the first general use of the new art of printing; and then, in the third place, the Bible. This book proved to be the most effective tool for the expansion of the Reformation movement. Luther translated it vividly and masterfully into German; and others followed with translations into the other tongues of Europe. Thus it became the basis of preaching and the source of catechetical instruction everywhere.

Once he had achieved fame as a reformer who commanded a large following, many approached Luther proposing schemes and devices and special programs of action—political men, ecclesiastical planners, soldiers and, of course, revolutionaries of many sorts. He rejected them all, saying that he was called by God to be an evangelist, responsible only for the souls of men, and that he would have nothing to do with programs designed to bring about changes in society. When he was confronted with the question of how room was to be made in the world for the truth which he had rediscovered and which all men needed to receive, he replied (and this remained his slogan throughout his life and served as the distinctive guide of action also among his followers and successors): "The Word must do it."

The fact that throughout his career he was sure that he was correct in this is an indication of the amazing naïveté and impracticality that characterized him. So he could say, "All that I have done is to set forth, preach, and teach God's Word. Otherwise I have done nothing. Thus while I slept, or while I had a glass of beer with my friend Philip and with Amsdorf, the Papacy was weakened as it never was previously by the action of any prince or emperor. I have done nothing.

The Word has done and accomplished everything. I just let the Word do its work." He felt that all that needed to be done in order to make the message of the Bible effective was to preach it and teach it in tracts, hymns, and catechisms. This is how the Lutheran Reformation got wings.

In the course of time, it obtained the support of the political rulers. They alone had the power through which a program of reform could be enacted. The most effective among them were the magistrates of the free towns; they enjoyed a certain freedom of action by virtue of which they could take into account the real and immediate concerns of the common people.

In this connection, we must note that, especially in the beginnings, Luther and his fellow reformers expected to draw the laity into an active participation in the regulation of church affairs. Luther even went so far as to propose that the congregations should have the right to call and institute and, if necessary, to dismiss their preachers. And, indeed, there developed, wherever the Reformation spread, a new kind of churchmanship. But on the whole, the common people were not yet ripe for the practice of congregationalism. In the course of time, some of the laity—princes, magistrates, lawyers, teachers, and generally, the educated—came to exercise a greater influence in the life of the church than laymen had ever been granted before (except under wholly different circumstances in apostolic times), but the "common man" remained excluded from any kind of church leadership and was forced to stay at the receiving end of clerical ministrations.

So when the peasants, inspired by the teachings and actions of Luther and his fellow reformers, took destiny in their own hands and revolted in order to recover their old rights and privileges—for theirs was a revolt with a backward look insofar as they aimed at the restoration of the "good old days" —they were slapped down, and ruthlessly so. Moreover, when some among the laity, interpreting the gospel in their own ways, began to inject considerable diversity into the new talk about the Christian faith, when as Luther put it, many individual prophets began to "buzz around," then they were pushed aside and ordered to follow the common course and not to disturb the public peace! It was in reaction to all this that there were formed, surprisingly quickly, the creedal churches of the Reformation. Organized by political action and instituted as authoritarian religious bodies, these territorial churches, under the leadership of the secular rulers, enforced creedal conformity; they were intolerant and exclusive of diversity.

Finally, then, what were the effects of the Reformation? We can speak about this much more readily today than its own contemporaries could. We can see today that the Reformation brought about a simplification of religion.

This simplification was fourfold. Instead of depending upon the authority of the Papacy and the priesthood, that is to say, upon the complex hierarchical institutionalism of the Roman Church and on conformity with the laws and regulations of old times, the reformers declared the Scripture alone to be the norm and source of the Christian life. The Scripture alone should be the spring on which the Christian lives. The Biblicism which now came into being was tantamount to a tremendous reduction of the religious authority which people had to follow. To be sure, the reformers advanced a remarkable understanding of the nature of the Scripture: They called it the Word of God, believing that God himself speaks from the words of Scripture to those who read or hear it, and they were certain that the Bible has a clear, simple meaning which immediately conveys itself to the minds of men. As Luther put it: *"Scriptura sui ipsius interpres*—the Scripture is its own interpreter."

It should not surprise us that the several reformers came to exhibit great diversities in the way in which they understood and applied the Scripture in the realms of doctrine and church order, daily life and Christian work. They were so baffled by this consequence of their proposition that the Scripture was simple and easily understood, that they were unable to come to terms with it. Hence they became exclusivistic toward one another and began to condemn one another: Lutherans pounced upon Zwinglians and Anglicans; Zwinglians upon Lutherans; Calvinists and Lutherans upon Anglicans; and all the major reformed churches—Lutherans, Calvinists, and Anglicans together—upon the Anabaptists. Each group of them, Lutherans, Zwinglians, Calvinists, Anglicans, as well as the Anabaptists, believed to rely upon the Scripture alone, sure that it could have only one true meaning. Strange!

Christianity was simplified also by the broad rejection, which in certain cases was conservative and in others radical, of ceremonialism. "A Christian," Luther said, and all the others repeated this after him, "lives by grace alone and not by any good work." Grace was understood as the merciful goodness of God as it is manifested in Christ. It was taken to be God's Spirit, the manifestation of his goodness. According to Roman Catholic understanding, by contrast, grace was a medicine, a healing power, obtainable through sacraments and religious ritual.

Under the impact of the Reformation, Christianity came to be deceremonialized and spiritualized. The outwardness of ritual was replaced by the inwardness of confidence in the renewing power of the merciful goodness of God. Henceforth, character and disposition were assigned primary importance in the Christian life in preference to works and actions, according to Luther's oft-repeated saying, "Good works do not make a man good, but a good man does good works." The Christian religion ceased to be primarily a rite. It became a faith.

The Christian was now seen as a person of faith, one ready to take a chance with the promise exhibited in Christ. He regards Christ as absolutely trustworthy; to him he surrenders; on him he stakes his life; he depends on Christ alone. This is the nature of faith, according to the understanding of the reformers. No man can hope to make himself acceptable in God's sight by his own works, activities, or enterprises. The Christian lives in the sight of God only by trusting with his whole person in the promises which God has declared to those through whom he has chosen to speak, particularly through Jesus Christ, in whom he disclosed himself personally.

All that was meant by this reliance upon Scripture alone, and upon grace alone, and upon faith alone, must be carried out, so the reformers believed, in the common life. Every person must learn that whatever he finds he has to do in his prescribed daily round constitutes a task which God calls him to perform. Wherever a person finds himself, there he must give expression to the living truth of the Christian faith. Wherever he finds himself, he must understand his work among his fellow men as a vocation, a divine calling. It was by this means that the reformers hoped confidently to transform human existence into a Christian order of life. It was in dependence upon this spirit of vocation that, so they felt, they would be able to bring about a transformation of civilization by the gospel far exceeding all that had been accomplished in preceding ages.

As we look upon the achievements of Protestantism, in the common life of the last centuries, we must say that much of what the reformers anticipated has indeed been fulfilled, although, on the one hand, they were much too confident that human life can be transformed quickly and, on the other hand, too much bound to the ways of established doctrines and conventions, at any rate to a greater degree than they themselves realized.

Furthermore, as we today consider the Reformation, we cannot but be impressed by the fact that its course and its actual accomplishments were far different from what people who in earlier times had looked forward to a radical renewal of life had expected.

Perhaps this is something to ponder for us who, as many believe, also live in an age of prereformation: Should a reformation of the church (or of life generally) actually come, it may be far different from what we are now able to anticipate.   HNW

3. Confronting the Modern World: The Last 150 Years

ROBERT T. HANDY

I

The phrase "the modern world" conjures up in one's mind many diverse and sometimes conflicting ideas. In one of his recent essays, Professor Hendrik Kraemer refers to "the vague, but very pregnant term, 'the modern world.' "[1] We must not pause long in the effort to define so vague an expression, lest we fail to get to our main theme of Christianity confronting that modern world. But we all know that the modern world is one of rapid transformation in almost all departments of life, rapid and ever accelerating transformation. Just half way through the last 150 years, in 1885, Dr. Josiah Strong wrote these words:

Any one as old as the nineteenth century has seen a very large proportion of all the progress in civilization made by the race. When seven years old he might have seen Fulton's steamboat on her trial trip up the Hudson. Until twenty years of age he could

(44)

TRACTOR   AIRPLANE
HARVESTER   AUTOMOBILE
                 RADIO
                 TELEPHONE
                 INCANDESCENT LAMP = 1879

not have found in all the world an iron plow. At thirty he might have traveled on the first railway passenger train. . . . For the first thirty-three years of his life he had to rely on the tinder-box for fire. He was thirty-eight when steam communication between Europe and America was established. He had arrived at middle life (forty-four) when the first telegram was sent. . . . Our century has been distinguished by a rising flood of inventions. The English government issued more patents during the twenty years succeeding 1850 than during the two hundred and fifty years preceding.[2]

The rising flood of inventions has continued to swell, and at an accelerating rate. All this has greatly stepped up the tempo of life in modern times as compared with earlier periods. As one Seminary dean stated it:

Steam and electricity have tremendously increased the pace of life. Everybody is in a hurry. . . . St. Martha is the patron saint of the women, and St. Vitus of the men. Nervous prostration is our characteristic disease. Leisure is a word for whose meaning we consult the dictionary. In the clatter of the train, in the click of the keys at the telegraph office the spirit of the age finds speech.[3]

It is not much to our comfort to find that that paragraph was written sixty-five years ago, before the first airplane had flown, before the steadily increasing tempo of twentieth-century life had begun. As we look backward, the pace of life in the 1890's seems leisurely indeed!

If we had to single out one factor in explanation of this modern world of ours, I suppose we should say science, both pure and applied; science, and its application to life through technology. For the nineteenth century saw the rapid rise of the achievements and of the prestige of science. Largely because of science, the nineteenth century experienced a whole network of revolutions in man's thought about himself, his past, and his world. Technology, as has been suggested in the quotations, altered the daily patterns of life not only in Europe and America but, through its ability to cross difficult barriers of time and space, all around the world.

At the beginning of this period of 150 years many areas of the world were little known, even vast continents; neither pole had been reached, nor had the highest mountains been climbed; much of the American continent was wilderness. How rapidly have the changes come; how quickly the blank spaces on the map filled in with exquisite detail!

As the world has become better known, it has also become far more heavily populated. Among the many revolutions of the last 150 years has been the sanitary revolution, which has allowed many infants who once would have died to live, and lengthened life expectancies impressively. In the long history of mankind the population did not reach the total of one billion until about 1833; it reached its second billion in 1933 and it is estimated that it will pass it third billion in 1963.[4] The utterly vast needs of such unprecedented masses have imposed an irritating and insistent strain on our economic and political processes and structures. There has been a steadily enlarging population throughout our period, but also an increasingly more mobile one. The nineteenth century saw vast migrations, such as those which filled the American west; the twentieth has witnessed the startling increase of an almost perpetual mobility as people restlessly travel, finding it possible to go farther and faster each year. When, in the middle of our period, Jules Verne wrote his fabulous *Around the World in Eighty Days,* it was considered the wildest kind of science fiction, but the time is down now almost to eighty minutes by space capsule. Increased mobility has allowed many families to change their places of residence with surprising frequency, so that a sense of rootlessness and impermanence arises.

The deeper revolutions have been in the realms of thought, for under the drive of scientific thinking long and tenaciously held ideas broke up like the ice on the river in spring. Every kind of scholarship was invaded; historians, for example, began to apply scientific method to the understanding of the past with amazing results. At Johns Hopkins the famous historian Herbert Baxter Adams transformed his seminar into a laboratory and "passed historical sources to and fro like rocks, fossils, or chemicals."[5] When sacred writings were also inspected with scientific detachment, the strain was too intense for many a devout soul who tried to hold his old faith in a revolutionary modern world but who could do so only by taking refuge in the past. Many a less devout soul drifted off into a vague humanism or practical secularism.

Looking at his native country a dozen years ago, Sir Walter Moberly was forced by the evidence he saw to conclude that

. . . the British nation is vastly less Christian than it used to be. It has undergone a drastic, and ever accelerating, process of secularizing. The traditional order of life, as it existed for instance for the villagers of Gray's *Elegy* and for countless earlier and several later generations, has been disrupted. Church and churchyard have lost their pivotal position. . . . For the common mind indeed "Nature" has silently displaced God as the ultimate basis to which all other things are referred.[6]

Such reflections as these recall to our minds some of the things we associate with that vague but pregnant phrase, "the modern world."

MSS-VSS
EPIGRAPHIC
NON-EPIG.

THE MIRACLE DRUGS

E = MC$_2$

TV

SPACE RESEARCH

II

When Christianity confronted this new world at the beginning of its modern period, it faced it with considerable courage and confidence, and with a surge of vitality set out to win it. For the first hundred years of the period, it was making progress in a remarkable way. Western and Protestant Christianity especially flourished, for the nineteenth century marked the high tide of the impact of European culture on the world. The nineteenth century saw Western modes of thought and life, with their heavy emphasis on democracy, education, and progress, vitally influencing the world. Protestant Christians especially felt an affinity for democracy, education, and progress. They believed that democracy as it was being developed was "an attempt, on the part of men, to deal with one another in a way that is consonant with the way in which God deals with them."[7] They contributed significantly to the rise of the educational level at home and abroad, planting thousands of schools and hundreds of colleges. They coupled a belief in the progress of civilization with the doctrine of God's providence in a way that may seem to us naïve, but which gave them a great sense of confidence and destiny. Older concepts of Christendom with established churches and medieval restrictions they saw as being replaced with a newer, freer, finer concept of Christendom which allowed for greater freedom and hope for individuals, encouraged the rise of many free churches which were in a generally friendly relation to other churches, and promoted the handling of the world's ills through voluntary action by men of good will. But it was a concept of Christendom still, with churches understood as intimately interrelated to the culture of which they were a part.

The churches often saw themselves as the best part of that culture, perhaps, but very much in tune with it and rarely over against it. It was a partnership of enlightened civilization, free states, and free churches. Of course, newly opened territories were understood to need the tutelage of the advanced nations. The great hope was that enlightened, Western, Christian civilization would soon spread its benevolent effects over all the world. A century and a half ago many preachers were putting into their sermons such statements as this: "May we not then yield ourselves to the confidence that Zion has seen her darkest hour, and that her light will henceforth continue to shine with increasing brightness to the perfect day?"[8] The Roman Catholic Church, as is well known, was having difficulty in coming to terms with the general liberal and democratic trends of the nineteenth century, which was in certain respects a Protestant century. But all Christian churches of the West saw the opportunities provided by the spread of their civilization around the world, and they labored, sometimes together, sometimes apart, sometimes in tension, to win the world for Christ and his church.

As the boundaries of civilization were steadily pushed back in the nineteenth century, the church was there. The modern foreign-missionary movement was touched off by the world vision of William Carey in the last decade of the eighteenth century. In the whole story of Christianity on the march, the nineteenth was indeed "the Great Century," as Kenneth Scott Latourette has so aptly named it in his massive seven-volume *A History of the Expansion of Christianity*. He devotes no less than three of the seven volumes to the varied and impressive nineteenth-century developments, dating the Great Century as the years from 1815-1914. Technological improvements made possible the opening of the dark places of the world, but missionary enthusiasm often sent pioneers on ahead, harbingers of both Christianity and civilization. So at the end of the century Christianity was really a world-wide movement, with outposts everywhere.

Nineteenth-century Christianity not only faced an expanding world as the boundaries were pushed back, but also confronted an enlarging world as population rapidly increased. However, in every land in Christendom there were elements in the population, often minority groups of one kind or another, which had not been effectively reached by the churches. So inner, home, or domestic mission movements were launched, and intensive evangelistic efforts to reach the unchurched were made. In some cases they were highly successful numerically; in the United States the percentage of church members in the total population has strikingly increased throughout the entire 150 years of this period.

But an inescapable part of industrial civilization is the great city with its huge concentration of population and its burgeoning social problems. It was soon discovered that old concepts about the inevitability of economic laws were outmoded, and that man could exercise control over his new urban environment. As Waldo Beach has pithily summed it up, "The realization of the fluidity of social structures and the capacity of man to alter his political and social environment is a nineteenth century insight."[9] As this realization came home to Christians, it helped to stimulate Christian social movements. Such movements represented the effort of Christians to deal significantly and Christianly with the human problems of the technological age. The social gospel, as presented so eloquently in America by Walter Rauschenbusch a half century ago, can be understood as part of the pattern of nineteenth-century Christendom, part of the effort to keep church and culture continuously related by both Christianizing the society and socializing the churches. Within their own frame of reference, Roman Catholics addressed the social question classically in Pope Leo XIII's important encyclical of 1891, *Rerum novarum.*

The churches not only faced the fact of larger populations with their problems; they also confronted the realities of mobile populations. New ways of reaching people on the march had to be discovered: Such things as camp meetings, circuit riders, chapel cars, railroad YMCA's, Sunday school missionaries, chaplains, and settlement houses remind us of what were originally imaginative efforts, many of them successful, to evangelize a procession.

The church also attempted to come to terms with the intellectual revolutions of the nineteenth century, revolutions linked with the spread of Darwinism and historical criticism, but the intellectual achievements were less impressive than the missionary, evangelical, and institutional successes. Some Christians did succeed in restating the gospel in the language and concepts of the modern world. But others became so enamored with the authority of science and with belief in the primacy of fact that the authority of revelation and belief in the primacy of faith lost its hold over them, and their religious ideas were recast in a humanist or naturalist frame of reference. At the other extreme were those who repudiated the intellectual achievements of the modern world, and denied the insights of theories of evolution and the results of biblical criticism. Often they made full use of the technological achievements of the modern world, but rejected certain of its intellectual achievements. This tendency to accept the technical advances but to retreat before revolutions in thought was already in evidence early in this period. As the

John Herman Randalls, father and son, put it many years ago:

Western society confronted the disruptive forces of science and the machine with a religious life strangely divided. On the side of moral and social ideals and attitudes, of the whole way of living which it approved and consecrated, Christianity had already come to terms with the forces of the modern age. . . .

On the side of beliefs, however, Christianity in the early 19th century had not come to terms with the intellectual currents of Western society.[10]

Both those who were engulfed by modern modes of thought and those who refused to come to terms with them contributed indirectly to the spread of secular modes of thought and life, the first by weakening Christian foundations, the second by presenting Christian faith in a way often unacceptable to thinking modern men. But Christians of various opinions did often overlook their intellectual differences in the continuing crusade for the Kingdom of God, the crusade for a Christian civilization and a Christian world. Beneath the surface was tension, but the crusade was succeeding and differences could be kept in their place. To focus on the United States for a moment, we find instructive the words of Gaius Glenn Atkins:

The first fifteen years of the twentieth century may sometime be remembered in America as the Age of Crusades. There were a superabundance of zeal, a sufficiency of good causes, unusual moral idealism, excessive confidence in mass movements and leaders with rare gifts of popular appeal. . . . The air was full of banners, and the trumpets called from every camp.[11]

So the nineteenth century was a Great Century for Christianity. I have mentioned Dr. Latourette's seven-volume *History of the Expansion of Christianity;* recently he has been writing another great series, on the theme *Christianity in a Revolutionary Age: A History of Christianity in the Nineteenth and Twentieth Centuries.* He argues, with impressive reference to an abundance of facts, that Christianity in Europe and beyond came to the close of the nineteenth century on a rising tide. Let me quote his own words from a summary at the end of the fourth volume:

> In the face of the challenge of revolutionary movements which had their inception in Western Christendom, which in part owed their existence to Christianity, and which appeared to imperil the continuation of that faith, and in spite of the fact that it seemed so closely integrated with the age which was passing that to many observers it appeared moribund, Christianity had a remarkable revival. At the close of the nineteenth century it was much more vigorous in the historic Christendom than it had been at the outset of that era and had spread more widely beyond the borders of its traditional centre than in any previous period. By the year 1914 it was more nearly global than it or any other religion had ever been. The revival had been in all three of the main branches of Christianity—Roman Catholic, Protestant, and Orthodox. It was most outstanding in Protestantism, was marked in the Roman Catholic Church, and, while less striking, was also apparent in various Orthodox bodies.[12]

Christianity was clearly on the march at the close of the first hundred years, two-thirds of the period we are considering. Western Christendom had been redefined for its encounter with the modern world, but the idea of Christendom, a Christian society and civilization the world over, persisted.

III

Then came the event that marked a decisive change in the story of the Christian encounter with the modern world, the First World War. Some have not hesitated to speak of the war and its aftermath as beginning the period of "the collapse of Western Christendom," meaning that Western Christendom began to lose its real essence and significance. Professor Hendrik Kraemer has stated in as clear a way as I have ever seen it put what a turning point the outbreak of world war in 1914 was:

It is a well-known fact that the first world war dealt an irreparable blow to the prestige of the West in the so-called "non-Christian" world. Up until that time, in spite of inner revolt against its dominating and domineering impact on the "East," Western culture and its principles had commanded high respect and enthusiastic assent among the intelligentsia of the Eastern countries, who constituted the vanguard of the nationalist movements and the efforts for radical self-reform. These Western principles were the dynamic instruments in their efforts. The suicidal European war of 1914-1918 destroyed this venerated image and caused deep disillusionment about the validity of Western culture. The inability of the West to avert a second world war and the very fact of the war, which drew the whole world into misery and destruction and saw the use of still more terrible means of annihilation, made this loss of prestige which, to the Easterner, if not to the Westerner, constitutes the collapse of the West. And not only of the West as a cultural image, but also of Western Christendom.[13]

For Americans, the deeper meaning of the outbreak of the First World War did not become clear until the Great Depression, the rise of Fascist and Communist dictators, and the outbreak of the Second World War. Professor Richard Hofstadter of Columbia University put it strikingly in the conclusion of his book on *The Age of Reform:*

The beginning of the [Second World] War meant that Americans, with terrible finality, had been at last torn from that habitual security in which their domestic life was merely interrupted by crises in the foreign world, and thrust into a situation in which their domestic life is largely determined by the demands of foreign policy and national defense. With this change came the final involvement of the nation in all of the realities it had sought to avoid, for now it was not only mechanized and urbanized and bureaucratized but internationalized as well. Much of America still longs for—indeed, expects again to see—a return of the older individualism and the older isolation, and grows frantic when it finds that even our conservative leaders are unable to restore such conditions.[14]

The year 1914 was the beginning of the end of the concept of Christendom in Western civilization. Many churches found themselves in cultural situations no longer congenial but sometimes hostile; many churches in Europe found themselves thrust into a political situation which forced them to resist or to surrender. The easy and free partnership between church and culture, which had marked much British and American Christianity especially, came to be challenged by many, though for conflicting reasons. Some outside the churches simply became hostile to religion, finding it an antiquated survivor from the past. Many churchmen saw that the churches had become ensnared by their enveloping cultures; they resisted attempts to exploit religious feelings and institutions for nationalistic purposes.[15] Latourette's summary of all this is sobering; let me quote a few more sentences from the compact conclusion of the fourth volume of his new series:

In the half-century which was ushered in by the fateful summer of 1914 Christianity was confronted with greater threats than it had known for many centuries. . . .

As a result of these threats and challenges, Christianity was losing whatever hold it had possessed on many millions in what had been known as Christendom. . . . The decline was most marked in the cities—whether London or Paris, Stockholm or Madrid, Hamburg or Marseilles, Berlin or Rome. . . . But it was also apparent in numbers of rural areas.[16]

But this, he adds, was only "one part of the picture." Christianity in the last fifty years of the period under consideration has been "very much alive" and in confrontation with the modern world. But its march has not been so much along the lines of geographical advance in alliance with its culture, but rather in certain significant new developments which may finally add up to a strikingly new period in the long history of the Christian Church. I would like to mention briefly seven such developments.

1. The famous World Missionary Conference met at Edinburgh in 1910 at a time when the forward march of the nineteenth century had not begun to falter; no one knew that four years later a fateful and stormy new period in the life of man was to explode on the world. But at that great gathering of a half-century ago were gathered up, commingled, and then released in what has become a great tide the streams of unitive Christianity. Roman Catholic theologian Gustave Weigel has called the Ecumenical Movement "undoubtedly the most striking ecclesiological event since the sixteenth-century Reformation."[17] Henry P. Van Dusen has spoken

forcefully of the "Ecumenical Reformation, a reformation in the twentieth century as radical and perhaps ultimately as far-reaching as the Protestant Reformation of the sixteenth century."[18]

Impelled both by recognition of the imperatives toward unity inherent in the Christian tradition and by the decline of the old ideas of Christendom, Christian churches have been drawing closer together. The movement itself has gone through the stages that many individual participants in it have gone through: after the initial flush of excitement comes the realization that the bringing together of churches of variant heritages and of differing national and cultural backgrounds is a painful as well as a challenging business. But possible disillusionment is checked by the deepening understanding that as we all, churches and Christians, draw nearer to Christ, we may draw nearer to each other.

The encounter of Christianity with the modern world has in the past half-century driven the churches deeper, driven them to ask searching questions, driven them to seek each other. Perceptive observers find that something very significant is happening. For example, when H. Richard Niebuhr studied theological education in this country he found that in their concern for the education of ministers, and one can add that this is true in other matters, the denominations "think of themselves increasingly as branches or members of a single community, as orders and institutions with special duties or assignments to be carried out in partnership with other branches of the one society. The idea of *Una Sancta,* of One Holy Church, is very pervasive despite relatively rare expression." In full awareness of the many exceptions, Niebuhr could conclude that "to the sympathetic observer the increasing unity of American Protestantism is more striking than its apparent diversity."[19] Increasing Christian unity is also steadily more striking and visible on the world scene, largely through the work of the World Council of Churches and through the witness of significant church unions.

2. Another important new development of the last half-century has been the theological revival. Whatever the achievements of the church in the nineteenth century, the close of that Great Century found a dangerous tension between the theological extremes, between modernists and fundamentalists, between experimentalists and traditionalists. This tension erupted in America as the bitter and debilitating fundamentalist–modernist controversy of the 1920's. But beginning with the work of Karl Barth, theological renewal movements that have cut across earlier stalemates have informed the whole Christian world. Dr. Truman B. Douglass has noted that something momentous is going on in the life of the church, for "theological work and biblical study are being carried on with a range and penetration not matched since the sixteenth century."[20] The withdrawal to the prayer cell, the study desk, the seminar room, the lecture hall may not seem to some to be Christianity on the march, but without devoted, patient, intelligent effort of this kind, hungry and often desperate men and women around the world will be lost to the cause of Christ, and will be claimed by other and rival faiths.

3. An important recent development which is being felt throughout the whole church is a new emphasis on the role and place of the laity. In many places now, such phrases as "the ministry of the laity" and "the people of God" (ò laós tôu theôu) have suddenly become alive with meaning. Professor Hendrik Kraemer has probably most cogently

and probingly stated the deeper dimensions underlying this important new development. He writes,

The responsible participation of the laity in the discharge of the Church's divine calling is not primarily a matter of idealism and enthusiasm or organizational efficiency, but of a new grasp of and commitment to the meaning of God's redemptive purpose with man and with the world, in the past, the present, and the future: a purpose which has its foundation and inexhaustible content in Christ, God incarnate, who died for us on the Cross and rose from the dead.[21]

The idea that all true Christians are in some sense ministers and that the role of the ordained clergy is to minister to ministers may yet release unexpectedly powerful forces hidden within our churches. Potentially, the Christian social movement can become alive in startlingly new ways, for laymen and laywomen have the technical knowledge needed for relevant social witness, and they live at the points of encounter of Christianity with culture.

4. The roots of the liturgical revival, to mention another development, of course go back far beyond the last half-century, but in recent decades the impact of the liturgical movement has been felt throughout the Christian world. Liturgical churches are recovering the deeper theological roots and meanings of their practices; nonliturgical churches are discovering that they have often let their biases screen them off from something that belongs to the gospel. In their emphasis on the words of God, some Protestants have not reflected much on the acts of God, saving acts which are represented in a dramatic and vivid way in the sacraments. The liturgical renewal has had much influence on the appearance of church buildings around the world, and more on

the shape of Christian worship from Sunday to Sunday.[22]

5. A development of the last half-century that Protestants may view with mixed feelings has been the surprising resurgence of Roman Catholicism. In the nineteenth century, that church opposed many of the cultural, political, and intellectual currents of the time, and often appeared to be in retreat before them even as she resisted them. But as many of the trends of nineteenth-century Western culture have run into tension and trouble, the centralized authority and massive stability of the Roman Catholic Church have made her appear impressive to some who had once been scornful. In a recent summary of the major developments in Catholic life and thought in the twentieth century, Professor Roger Aubert has called attention to a number of important internal developments: for example, the continued progress of the missionary movement, significant trends in the deepening of the inner life, the spread of the Marian movement (which, Aubert notes, "at times passes the bounds of moderation"[23]), the contribution of the liturgical movement, the vigor of the biblical movement which has led to something of a popular biblical awakening, the renewal of Christian education for children, the introduction of new forms of pastoral ministry, the promotion of the lay apostolate (including the remarkable development of Catholic Action), a theological ferment that has attempted seriously to deal with the modern mind, and the rise of Catholic ecumenism.[24] This latter, coupled with the Ecumenical Movement which has so engaged Protestants and Orthodox, has led at last to a quite new atmosphere in Catholic–Protestant relations, and a promising dialogue has been opened.[25]

6. Highly significant among the developments of the last half-century has been the rapid maturing of churches in

countries that were once missionary lands. Missionary outposts have been transformed into indigenous and flourishing
churches. These churches have shown decisively that the
Christian Church has not become merely Western, but is
truly universal. Perceptive observers saw that a half-century
ago at Edinburgh, for one of them wrote:

> But possibly the most interesting, certainly by far the most
> significant figures of all, were those of the Oriental and African
> delegates, yellow, brown or black in race, that were scattered
> among the delegates in that World Conference. For not only by
> their presence but by their frequent contributions to the debates,
> they gave final proof that the Christian religion is now rooted in
> all those great countries of the Orient and the South; and not only
> so, but that it possesses in those countries leaders who, for intel-
> lectual stability and all-round competence, were fully worthy of
> standing by the men who have been mentioned, even without the
> traditions of two millenniums of western Christianity at the back
> of them.[26]

How prophetic those words, written fifty years ago! For
today some of the most hopeful efforts in church unity and
genuine evangelism come from churches that were not so
long ago missions. In providing genuinely creative leadership
for the church in this technological age, the last may indeed
become first.

7. Finally, no one can survey the story of Christianity's
march in the twentieth century even as swiftly as I have had
to do it without speaking of the deepened faith and authentic
insights that emerged out of the resistance of faithful Christians to the tyranny of European dictators. It was in 1934
that a group of Christian leaders of Germany at Barmen took
their stand against the encroachments of the state, and said
emphatically:

Jesus Christ, as He is testified to us in Holy Scripture, is the one Word of God, whom we are to hear, whom we are to trust and obey in life and in death.

We repudiate the false teaching that the church can and must recognize yet other happenings and powers, images and truths as divine revelation alongside this one Word of God, as a source of her preaching.[27]

These men saw that Christendom was breaking up, and they stated afresh the only ultimate standing ground for Christians. Their spirit flamed into the church resistance movement against Hitler, was carried into the sturdy *Kirchentag* and Evangelical Academy movements in Germany, and lives on among many who now face Communist control.

IV

Over the last 150 years, then, the church has faced the modern world, that world marked by the dramatic and revolutionary impact of science and technology on human life and thought. For a hundred years, the encounter was successfully carried on in a usually free but significant partnership with many of the leading forces of Western civilization. Since 1914, the world picture has startlingly changed and the familiar patterns of Christendom have fast faded, but the march of Christianity has continued, along new, often tortuous, less traditional paths. But the period as a whole has been a remarkable one. Henry P. Van Dusen in his forceful way has summed it up in these words:

By any reasonable calculus that might be proposed, the period of which we are immediate heirs—roughly the last one hundred and fifty years from the dawn of the nineteenth century to mid-

THE MARCH OF FAITH: WE GARRISON

point in the twentieth—was the epoch of largest, most varied, and most notable Christain achievement in the nearly two millenniums of Christian history.[28]

But where are we today? This is the theme of the next chapter.

PART II

CHRISTIANITY TODAY

4. Christianity Today: An Eye-Witness Report

HENRY P. VAN DUSEN

I

On the afternoon of Sunday, November 19, 1961, some 1,500 persons converged upon the Vigyan Bhavan, the superbly appointed Conference Hall erected by the government of India in its capital city of New Delhi. They came, men and women, from every continent and some seventy countries, almost as many as the United Nations, for the opening session of the Third Assembly of the World Council of Churches.

Any event which is not just a fleeting happenstance is more than the occasion itself. It gathers into itself a vast accumulation of earlier events which have led up to and determined it; and it stretches forth in an outflow of events which issue from it and which it determines. Like a human person, it is the child of an innumerable ancestry and derives its character from them; it begets an unnumbered posterity and implants its character upon them. It is the heir of the ages and the parent of ages yet unborn.

Formally, the New Delhi Assembly was a periodic legislative session of the World Council of Churches. In fact, it was far more than that. It was the climax, the end result, and the symbol of the most significant developments within Christendom in modern times. More particularly, it marked the confluence of two great streams of historic church life which have been flowing in ever larger volume and with accelerating momentum through the past century and a half. Each of those streams, in turn, embraces the coalescence of unnumbered rivulets which arose in diverse circumstances and varied places across the earth's surface in the last hundred and fifty years. One stream is the Modern Missionary Movement; the other, the contemporary Movement for Christian Unity. Their confluence at New Delhi was both symbolized and actualized in an act effected in the very first moments of the Assembly—the "integration" of the two world bodies which respectively channeled these two streams, the International Missionary Council and the World Council of Churches, into an enlarged World Council of Churches. This union, consummated at the beginning of the Assembly, was, in the judgment of many, not only its most important action; it was the most significant single event in Christendom since the formal creation of the World Council of Churches at its First Assembly in Amsterdam in 1948. Behind this act lay a century and a half of Christian history.

II

The fabled visitor from Mars who had chanced upon this planet at the dawn of the nineteenth century would hardly have entertained good hopes for the future of Christianity. For more than a century previous, in both faith and life the Christian Church had suffered deepening strain, sterility, and loss. In area after area of the world's life to which Christian missionaries had ventured in the preceding era of vigor and extension, their struggling young churches had died or shriveled to almost nothing. In Japan, Christianity had been driven wholly underground. In China and India, it struggled to maintain a precarious toe-hold. The vast continent of Australia and New Zealand and most of the Pacific islands were as yet wholly untouched by Western culture and Western religion. Around the African seacoasts could be discovered a few small and seemingly unimportant Christian outstations. Moreover, Christian missions of that epoch were usually spiritual adjuncts of European political and economic domination. Christianity was still quite definitely a Western faith. Its fate as a world religion appeared linked to the future of European conquest.

Even in Europe and America, however, the Christian churches were suffering sharp retreat. In Europe this was the age of Rationalism and Romanticism, when the prophets of doom for Christianity raised powerful voices, especially influential with labor and the intellectuals. Many Americans hold a mistaken view of the strength of religion at the time of the founding of their nation. To be sure, the early settlers had come largely from Christian motives. But by the time of the Revolution and the Constitution, the church had sunk to a level of relative impotence. There is a famous item in the annals of Yale College that in the year 1800 not a single student could be discovered who would admit that he was a Christian. Yet, then as now, Yale was not notably more pagan than its principal rivals.

Such were the conditions and outlook for Christianity at the beginning of the nineteenth century. Our hypothetical man from Mars, as he prepared to return to his planetary habitat, might well have left a message of condolence for a religion which had once appeared to promise much, but which at that day seemed fated for inconsequence and possibly for extinction.

Now let us imagine this same Martian traveler—or his great-great-grandson—returning to Earth in the mid-twentieth century. Christianity has become the professed faith of the Western Hemisphere—the vast continents of North and South America with their populations of some 250 million people. In the Pacific basin, the continent of Australia and New Zealand and many of the lesser islands are inhabited by predominantly Christian populations. In Africa, Christianity has worked inland from the seacoasts to establish sizable and vigorous churches among almost all the native tribes. Indeed, at least some beginnings of a firmly founded indigenous church are to be discovered in every principal country on the face of the earth. Perhaps most noteworthy of all, among the most advanced peoples of Asia, those most deeply rooted in ancient and mature Oriental cultures—India, Japan, China —the Christian Movement, although numbering in its membership an insignificant minority of their populations, is now flourishing under the ever more vigorous leadership of native Christians whose influence upon national thought and life is out of all proportion to their numbers.

No other movement in human history has advanced so far or so fast in so short a space of time. No other movement has ever won the adherence of so many or so large a proportion of mankind—today, about 850,000,000 or roughly one-third of humanity. Thus Christianity has become, for the first time, a world religion, the first world faith our planet has known.

Implicit in that fact are two others. Christianity has become potentially a universal faith, a faith for all humanity; for it has demonstrated its power to win the spontaneous and convinced allegiance of all sorts and conditions of persons— men, women, and children of every race and nation, from every type of cultural background, and at every level of cultural advance. And the Christian Church has become potentially a world community, a living and multiplying fellowship of peoples from the whole earth—in contrast to the League of Nations and the United Nations, a true world community—the first to take shape among mankind.

III

If that same visitor from Mars at the dawn of the nineteenth century had been interested in Christian unity, he might have traveled the earth from end to end and from pole to pole, visiting every continent and country, every city, village, and hamlet, without discovering more than one or two instances of Christians of different Communions coming together across denominational lines even for fellowship or consultation.

Today he would find uncounted thousands of transdenominational bodies, all the way from Councils of Churches in nearly one thousand cities and towns in the United States and increasing numbers in other countries, through National Councils of Churches in seventy lands, and scores of interdenominational bodies concerned with education, medicine, theological training, agriculture, social service, publication, mass media, to several world Christian organizations—a vast and intricate structure of consultation and co-operation reaching its climax in the two bodies, the World Council of Churches and the International Missionary Council, which joined at New Delhi to form the copestone of Christian unity. And he would learn that, in contrast to *one* church union in the preceding eighteen centuries, this same period of little more than a century has recorded no fewer than one hundred organic unions of previously separated national church bodies. He would be told that the most notable of these "union churches" have been achieved not in Europe or America where Christianity has existed for centuries, but in Asia where the church has come into being in the past century and a half: the Church of Christ in Japan, the Philippines, China, Thailand, North India, and, probably the most noteworthy, the Church of South India.

These are among the facts which have led one of the most distinguished political scientists of the English-speaking world, Sir Ernest Barker of Cambridge University, to declare: "Our century has its sad features. But there is one feature in its history which is not sad. That is the gathering tide of Christian union"; and the late Archbishop of Canterbury, William Temple, to hail Ecumenical Christianity as "the great new fact of our era . . . one great ground of hope for the coming days." For it is these two developments together— the Christian world mission and the movement for Christian unity—which constitute Ecumenical Christianity, a movement both world-wide and united. It is these two developments which are increasingly spoken of as the Ecumenical Reformation, thus defined by one of its youthful leaders: "It is a Reformation which amid the provincialism of the churches asserts the world mission of the church. It is a Reformation which amid the disunity of the churches asserts the unity of the church."[1] I have elsewhere ventured to describe it as "a Reformation in the twentieth century as radical and perhaps ultimately as far-reaching as the Protestant Reformation of the sixteenth century,"[2] a judgment shared by one of the best-informed Roman Catholic students of the subject: " 'The ecumenical movement' has brought changes in religious thinking comparable to the changes caused by the Reformation of the sixteenth century."[3] This is the reality which found institutional expression and its most vivid and dramatic demonstration at New Delhi in November and December of 1961 in the Third Assembly of the World Council of Churches.

IV

Christianity on the march today! How shall we envision it?

Seven times in the past quarter-century, I have had the rare privilege of seeing something of the world Christian Movement at first hand—on every continent (except Antarctica!) and in over sixty countries.

Twenty-five years ago, my wife and I made a leisurely eight-month serpentine circuit of the globe, largely by ship—from Los Angeles down the Pacific with brief stops in Honolulu, Fiji, and Samoa, and on to New Zealand and Australia; then northward through the Netherlands East Indies (now Indonesia) to Singapore, Hong Kong, Manila, and Japan; next, overland through Korea and Manchuria to China—north, east, south, central, and west China, at the darkest hour of her life-struggle with Japan; on through Indo-China and Siam (Thailand) and Burma to India for the World Missionary Conference at Madras; and, on the way home, short stops in Egypt, Palestine, and Europe.

Fourteen years later, I again circled the globe, this time wholly by plane—around the world in sixty days, outspeeding Jules Verne's imaginary journey of the last century, *Around the World in Eighty Days*, which so delighted our grandparents by its fantastic absurdity: from Seattle "north to the Orient" to Japan; thence southward to Formosa (Taiwan), the Philippines, Indonesia, Singapore, Bangkok, and on to Lucknow, India, for a fortnight's meetings of the World Council of Churches' Central Committee; next, resuming flight, past Karachi to Cairo, gateway to Africa; then, a four-week circuit of the African continent down the east coast via Uganda and Kenya and Rhodesia to Johannesburg; next, turning northward and homeward, along the west coast—the Congo, the Cameroons, Nigeria and the Gold Coast (Ghana); a brief stop in Lisbon, and so home.

Again, in late 1961 and early 1962, my wife and I completed another plane circuit, touching many of the same lands and places: New York to Honolulu to Japan to Taiwan to Manila to Hong Kong to Singapore to Bangkok to Rangoon to New Delhi and the World Council Assembly; on its conclusion, a brief holiday in Nepal; and then, in a single night, from beyond India's northernmost boundary in Nepal to close to India's southernmost tip in Kerala, home of Asia's two most ancient churches, dating at least from the fourth century, on the historic Malabar coast; thence, via Bangalore and Bombay to Karachi and Beirut and again Cairo; then, five weeks in Africa-south-of-the-Sahara via Addis Ababa, Nairobi, and Salisbury to Victoria Falls; a short week in South Africa; the Rhodesias, Kenya, Tanganyika, and Uganda; thence across to the west coast—Nigeria and Ghana —and Scotland and home.

In the intervening years, I had been back to China briefly

at war's end in 1946 and to Ghana in West Africa for a three-week conference in 1958; also, twice to South America: first, along its northern littoral; and then around that continent—Brazil and Uruguay, the Argentine, Peru and Ecuador.

Altogether, seven fairly wide-ranging journeys to Asia, Africa, Oceania, and Latin America. Impressions, illustrations, and interpretations will be drawn from all seven trips.

V

The Christian World Movement. How shall one describe it? There is space to mention only two or three of its most characteristic and important features.

First of all, the many-sided, comprehensive, rounded character of that Movement as one finds it in Asia and Africa and Oceania and Latin America—what we speak of as the "lands of the Younger Churches."

Presumably, no one today is so benighted, out-of-date, as to harbor the dog-eared picture of the Christian missionary as a well-intentioned but rather commonplace preacher, clad in a long frock coat, standing under a palm tree, a Bible in one hand and an umbrella in the other, exhorting half-naked savages to discard their heathen ways and accept the Christian God. That caricature had best be relegated to the attic along with our childhood toys and youthful fantasies of the man in the moon.

But if, as we try to visualize a Christian Center overseas, we think of the local church we know best at Main and Market streets, lifted bodily and planted somewhere in Asia or Africa, though reduced to the elementary proportions and program appropriate to primitive conditions and peoples, that conception likewise requires radical reconstruction. If we are to think realistically, that is, in accordance with facts, we must imagine not only a local church but the entire local school system, and the local hospital and its medical staff, and all of the community's social services transplanted abroad; but all of them organic parts of one unified agency.

The typical Christian Center, whether in an Asian city or in an African jungle, is not simply a church or the shade of a palm tree as improvised substitute. It is a center of three or four buildings—church, school, hospital—from which a team of co-workers with varied gifts and equipment—a doctor and nurses, a highly trained linguist, a school superintendent and teachers, an agriculturist, a social worker, *and* a minister —move out into the community and its environs in manifold helpfulness to all, whatever their race or religion, who need and will accept their ministry. All are services of a church which, almost everywhere today, is under the leadership of Christians of that land.

Here is the testimony of the most recent authoritative study of tropical Africa, sponsored by the Twentieth Century Fund:

The Influence of the Christian Church

Imponderables are always troublesome. Faith cannot be priced; the impact of a sermon, spoken or lived, cannot be measured. And because they are troublesome, there is a rather natural tendency to underrate them, if not to ignore them. But to do this with the influence of the Christian church on the community life of tropical Africa would be quite wrong for several reasons. In the first place, every mission station has been the nucleus of a community (often a very small one) and a nucleating agent since missions began, which was long before most governments and corporations began. In the second place, the secular agencies have generally taken the view that the church was a useful aide-de-camp to be taken along wherever they went, to deal with all those awkward matters for which they had neither the time nor the understanding. In the third place, there are about 20 million Africans who call themselves Christians, who belong to one or other of the confessions, and who, in greater or less measure, live by what they confess. And in the fourth place, the churches have shown that while they have no monopoly of community spirit, their best variety of it retains its potency longer than most. . . .

Consider, for instance, the kind of thing a well-equipped bush mission station does. It runs a school, where the children of the district learn not only to pray and sing but also to read, write and calculate, and where they encounter, for the first time in all likelihood, the notion that all people are not as they are—that there are different ways of looking at life, of spending one's energies and one's leisure. It runs a medical center, to which all who have need of doctoring, nursing, injections and drugs may come, whether they are members of the mission church or not. There they learn that sickness is a physical and psychological phenomenon, not the result of sorcery, witchcraft or "wishing" by ill-disposed persons; that it is possible to avoid about half of the customary sicknesses by keeping clean and about half of the rest by eating different foods and sleeping under a net. It runs a number of training programs, in farming and perhaps in printing, motor maintenance, carpentry and masonry, that open up possibilities of better living. It almost certainly runs a riot of recreations, from soccer and glee clubs to drumming and dominoes. And its doors are never closed to those seeking comfort or counsel, a go-between or a good listener.

The well-staffed, well-equipped urban mission station or church center is likely to offer even more in the way of community services—everything, in fact, from scout troops, sports clubs, sewing bees, pre-adolescent and premarital instruction groups, and pre-natal and postnatal clinics to adult school groups and classes for the training of church members as office holders, speakers and counselors. All of these services . . . will have this in common, that they bring together in intimate fellowship a group of people within or related to the total congregation in a way that meets a particular need of the group and fosters their identification with the total life of the church.

The churches, urban and rural, have served other secular functions, too. They have taught the Africans to raise and administer funds, to take care of property, to keep accounts, run committees, organize conferences and speak in public—in short, to take the kind of responsibility that is indispensable to the development of a democratically ordered community. . . .

No community having such a fellowship in its midst can expect to remain untouched by it. And since there are "fellowships"—congregations, assemblies, missions, etc.—in fully three fourths of tropical Africa, it is probably true that only in the solidly Islamic areas . . . are there any people who are not being touched by the Christian church. . . .

The kind of movement considered seeks, by doing a little for a lot of people, to tap the wellsprings of their desire for a better life and so get them to bestir themselves in their own behalf. That is, it is a pump-priming movement. . . . Of course, there is no telling what a primed pump will yield. . . . Most of the time, however, it is true to say that like yields like. Where the emphasis has been on spiritual gains—fredom from fear, superstition and tyranny, or greater happiness, dignity and decency—the yield tends to be strongly religious and political.

Its faults, limitations and failures notwithstanding, the Christian church must still be reckoned one of the great community-building and community-strengthening forces in tropical Africa.[4]

A "typical Christian mission."

There comes to my mind, irresistibly, my first exposure to such a mission, on one of the remote islands of the Netherlands East Indies (now Indonesia) in the summer of 1938.

If the eye runs across and down the map of Asia to its south-easterly tip at Singapore and then directly eastward, it will fall upon a chain of islands stretching across the Pacific a distance the width of the United States. Amongst that vast archipelago, microscopic examination of most world maps will detect a minute dot distinguishable by its peculiar shape like an octopus. Insignificant on a world scale, Celebes is an island of 40,000 square miles harboring at that time a population of some 3,000,000 Malayans, mostly people of very primitive life and culture.

For almost twelve hours with only a break for the night we motored up from Makassar, the principal commercial and political center, into the remote mountainous hinterland. Mile after mile the rough road picks its way along the scanty edge of precipitous cliffs, round hair-raising bends, up and up, with ever grander, wilder jagged peaks on either side. Our ancient Dodge bumped and swayed, shifting to second, to low, then back again, but pushed steadily forward and upward like a wiry kangaroo. For hours we saw no white face, heard no language other than Malay and the local dialects. As the scenery became wilder, so did the appearance and demeanor of the diminutive half-naked brown men and women along the road. Their rude rattan huts perched more and more insecurely on bamboo stilts. At the first sound of our car they leaped for the edge of the road and turned after us wild and stupid eyes in uncomprehending stares. A fine drizzle enveloped the mountains and added a slimy surface to the other hazards of this precarious highway.

Presently we noted several of the houses for which we had been told to watch, built in the very distinctive shape of the native ships or *praus* with high decks and great projecting bows and sterns which are such a marked feature of Makassar harbor. Houses constructed in this fashion with lofty overhanging roofs at each end present a most picturesque and attractive appearance. We knew we had come into the borders of the Toradja's territory. These tiny people (in stature a full foot below average height), driven two hundred miles into the interior centuries ago, had pushed their boats upstream before them and continue to build their homes in that distinctive shape and to bury their dead in *praus* hewn of wood or stone. Secure in their mountain fastnesses, nearly half a million of them, they have successfully resisted penetration by the stronger and fiercer tribes below. While the latter have been Muslims for centuries, the Toradja practise unaltered primitive animism and ancestor-worship. We passed their burial-places—caverns cut out of the solid face of rock-cliffs. Here their dead, after being kept a full year in the houses where they die—usually a single room which serves as dwelling for the entire family from great-grandparents to great-grandchildren—are finally laid away with orgiastic feasts and considerable promiscuity, but with superstitious beliefs about their continuing influence from the vivid spirit world.

At last the road wound down into a river-plain and we entered a typical village. But at the outskirts on either side was a grass-covered clearing. To the left, a brown steeple lifted above the trees revealing a little Dutch church. Beyond, a plain square building unmistakably announced the village school. A little farther on and across the road, a low one-storied white building suggested a hospital. In the doorway of the house just beyond, a young couple clad entirely in the white of the tropics smiled a characteristically Dutch welcome.

Both of our hosts had been leaders of the Dutch Student Christian Movement in undergraduate days. After medical course and internship in Holland and a couple of years of special preparation in tropical diseases in Java, he had come here as his first appointment. Before her marriage, she was a full graduate in theology at the University of Utrecht. Cocoa and cake helped to relax the strangeness of first meeting and refresh us after our journey. We discovered many mutual friends.

It was Sunday morning. As we had passed the little church we had noted several tardy worshippers slipping in, shielding themselves from the downpour with large banana leaves, Rante Pau's customary umbrella. We inquired if it were too late to join the worship. The doctor, explaining that it was a quarterly communion and in the Toradja dialect, said that he thought the service must be drawing toward its close since he had just heard the strains of the "middle hymn"—marking not the middle of the service, be it explained, but the middle of the sermon, with a good half hour of preaching on either side. We crossed the road, slipped into the church and stole forward into front pews as all others were crowded. The Dutch minister in black Geneva gown was reading his sermon in the vernacular. In the last ten minutes of an hour's carefully read discourse, one could not be certain that the auditors were grasping the full weight of its substance. There was no slackening of intent and reverent attention but I thought I detected a slight falling off in capacity for absorption during those closing paragraphs. However, one quickly sensed that the message of the worship was being conveyed, far more effectively than by spoken word, through the unadorned beauty of the building, through simple hymns to familiar tunes, through the indefinable intimacy of deep fellowship, perhaps most of all through the stillness which pervaded the church and all its company—simple, unemotional, genuine, comradely, reverent, moving. Presently the sermon was laid aside and, coming down from the pulpit, the minister took his place at the center of the long table spread the width of the church. After the lovely Dutch custom which so nearly reproduces the setting of the First Supper, the worshippers came forward and took their places seated at table to his right and left and the bread and cup were passed from hand to hand. Then one knew that Christian worship when true and sincere is essentially the same in every tongue and every clime, and that its focal center is in one place only—at the Supper of One who first took bread and broke it, and then rose from table and washed his friends' feet.

It was not until we took places at the table facing the congregation that we had our first opportunity really to see them. That sight will remain with me always. We looked out upon some three hundred little brown men and women and boys and girls, clean, alert, barefooted but well and becomingly dressed, spotless in their simple native costumes, hair immaculately arranged, winsome and charming, almost every face lighted by an eager sincere reverence and confident repose. The contrast to the unkempt bedraggled figures and the frightened staring faces which we had passed steadily for the preceding two days was overwhelming.

The external contrasts—in cleanliness, health, intelligence, happiness, freedom from fear—no one could miss. It was only later, when we visited huts of non-Christians, inspected collections of family fetishes, learned in detail of the beliefs and customs of animist worship and grasped something of the superstition and terror from which it springs, that the deeper contrasts could be fully appreciated. In their presence many of the discussions of Christian missions which one had heard and in which he had been a participant evaporated into irrelevance like mist at sunrise or certain "advanced" theories of marriage in the radiant serenity of a lovely home.

Since it was Sunday, the little schoolhouse was closed. It stood near by with its promise of the beginnings of education, and the release which education brings from tethering superstition and terror, for all who would come. We met the head of the school-system for that locality with responsibility for some sixty-five schools scattered through the mountains. Also the "language expert"—a brilliant linguist who was giving his life to the mastery of the native dialects in order that a door might be opened for these primitive peoples into the riches of mankind's learning and literature.

The doctor inquired if we cared to see the leper sanitarium. Our faces must have betrayed a slight hesitation for he reassured us that there was no danger of contagion. A half-mile back from the hospital, we suddenly came out upon a small plateau—to discover ourselves in one of the most altogether lovely villages we had ever seen. A dozen little homes, beautifully designed and constructed by local workmanship in the shape of the native *prau* and tastefully decorated by the lepers themselves, housed a hundred and ten lepers. Each doorstep was flanked by a colorful garden. The best sanitary arrangements prevented disease and furnished a demonstration in public health. From the hillside just above, a somewhat larger *prau* overlooked the community; it was the church. The whole suggested a garden-village. Again, the contrast to the crowded, tumble-down campongs through which we had been motoring was staggering.

We passed in and out among the residents. On one porch a leprous mother rocked a newborn infant. Before another, children played in the sand. Everywhere cheerful contented faces and cordial greetings welcomed us. We learned that the less severe cases can be cured. "But," I said, "there are no walls, no fences, no guards." The doctor smiled. "Of course not. No one wants to leave. If they were to return to their homes, they would be driven from their own villages, quite possibly they would be killed." Here was a leper colony which was not merely a haven of safety and happiness, offering treatment and possibly cure for over a hundred social outcasts, but also a model village for the entire locality!

It was late evening before we found time to visit the hospital itself. Darkness had fallen and the doctor and I felt our way around the dim wards by oil-lamplight. For there was no electricity, therefore no lighting-system, no drying facilities for bandages constantly wet in the humid dampness of the rainy season, above all no X-ray.

Here and there beneath a bed one or more figures were curled up on the floor. The doctor explained that they were members of the patient's family. Only on condition that they might accompany him would they permit their sick relative to enter the hospital. I was surprised to note that several beds were empty. But I was pointed to a figure stretched underneath. The patient could not rest comfortably on the unaccustomed luxury of a hospital cot so had rolled onto the floor and there slept peacefully!

Seventy beds, always overcrowded. For the constituency of that little hospital numbered 300,000 people. And the area of responsibility, close to 10,000 square miles of jagged mountains pierced by hardly a road. It had to be covered mainly on horseback, with a dozen dispensaries which supplement the work of the central hospital to be visited. The medical staff consisted of one doctor and one trained nurse, assisted by locally trained native helpers. Tuberculosis, venereal disease, leprosy, cholera, trachoma, rupture—these were the major ailments. The most crying need was an electric-plant, but that was a dream to conjure with for the future. When I was saying good night and laid on the table a small bill—less than an evening's theatre at home—the young doctor grasped my hand with tears in his eyes.

As we drove off in the gray dawn the following morning, our last glimpse of Rante Pau was of two dim figures standing in the doorway where they had greeted us the previous day, weary and a little haggard but still smiling. General practitioner, surgeon, obstetrician, ophthalmologist, orthopedist, tropical disease specialist, leprosy expert, friend-at-large to 300,000 primitive people!

This incident is not important primarily for itself, but as an illustration. In its main features—the human situation disclosed and the work of the Christian Church toward meeting that need —it could be multiplied many times from our very limited observations in this small corner of the world. The islands of Indonesia alone—60,000,000 people, half the population of the United States, vast numbers of them entirely without medicine, without education, without faith save for the work of the little Christian churches. None of those good things would be theirs until brought by the slow advance of Christian missions.

So much nonsense is talked about missions! I defy any one with open eyes and a modicum of concern for his fellow-men to confront life as it actually is for vast masses of humanity of primitive culture and religion, then witness a center of Christian faith and life among them, and still question the validity and immeasurable importance of the Christan Movement. It stands among these people absolutely alone—the only agency with a comprehensive strategy for the liberation, illumination, advancement of every aspect of their life.

As for opportunity for the enlistment of life with maximum usefulness and satisfaction, where else can an able and competently trained man or woman of medicine place his life so effectively? Where else can a teacher or minister or social worker hope to count for as much? The *one* medium of truth, education, healing, friendship, mediation, the compassion of Christ, the reality of God among a whole tribe or nation.[5]

The typical Christian center—a hospital, a school, a church. A *hospital!*

Long before governments and foundations turned *their* attention to the appalling physical needs of underdeveloped peoples, the Christian Church was bringing its ministry of health and healing. Indeed, governments, whether national or foreign, and philanthropy are building squarely on foundations laid decades ago by Christian missions. More than that, make no mistake; far beyond the outmost reach of government or private medicine today, the Christian doctor and Christian nurses are still pressing into the wilderness or jungle or city slum, with drugs and dispensaries, concern and kindliness, treatment and relief.

A single illustration from mankind's most dread disease. Mrs. Eleanor Roosevelt, speaking a few years ago to a conference of college girls on Christian vocations, told the incident of a young American woman who went to India for Point Four service. On the streets of Calcutta, she came upon a group of lepers, their toes and fingers, ears and noses eaten away by that repulsive malady. In horror, she shrank back and turned away with the cry, "I can't stand it; I'm going home." And she did. Mrs. Roosevelt did not go on to say that in every country on earth where leprosy has branded its victims accursed, it has been the Christian Church which has been first to bring haven and care; today, in many lands, it is still the only agency ministering healing and even cure. All over Asia and Africa, one finds Christian leprosy sanitaria, like the one in Rante Pau.

Of course, that is only the smallest and a very specialized part of Christian medicine. In New York City, there is one doctor for every four hundred residents. In certain remote areas of Asia and Africa, there is still one doctor per million people; and he is almost always a Christian missionary.

We went to Nepal for a holiday. While there, we came almost by chance upon two of the most remarkable missionary agencies in the world: a Protestant medical mission and a Roman Catholic educational program.

The United Mission to Nepal is the completely unified project of no fewer than seventeen missionary agencies from Japan, Australia, Norway, Sweden, and Scotland as well as from Canada and the United States, representing theological and denominational differences as wide as the Regions Beyond Missionary Union, the Bible and Medical Missionary Fellowship, the Central Asian Mission, the World Mission Prayer League (all strongly Fundamentalist) and American Methodists and Presbyterians, Anglicans, and the United Churches of Canada, India, and Japan. The staff is drawn from fifteen nations and over twenty denominations—probably the most widely ecumenical staff in the world (with the possible exception of the World Council of Churches in Geneva). They direct six hospital centers and clinics in eight different localities. Of course, what is of first importance and overwhelmingly impressive is the work itself: pioneering services to the health of an entire nation by a corps of highly trained and devoted doctors, nurses, and medical technicians, motivated by Christian compassion for elemental human need, yet prohibited by the laws of the country they serve from speaking of the gospel which has sent them and sustains them there. Here is as convincing a refutation of carping critics of "missions" as could be found anywhere in the world. But there is another significance. This is probably the most outstanding instance in the world of a form of Christian unity which has hardly been noted—a form which stands between "co-operation" and "church union"—the complete unification for a particular purpose of the resources in personnel and support of several different churches and missionary agencies, in this case of the most diverse national and theological loyalties. I have ventured to call this "confederation"[6] and to hail it as one of the most novel, profound, and promising examples of practical Christian unity anywhere in the world.

Today the Christian ministry of healing is largely through native doctors and nurses who have been taught by the missionaries. Some years ago, far up in the French Cameroon, I visited a Presbyterian hospital where, that morning, thirteen operations had been performed entirely by a corps of African surgeons, not one of whom had had an hour of formal medical education. I said to the missionary doctor who was my host, "Weren't you at hand to supervise or help," "No need," he replied. "They are far more skillful than we are."

2.

A hospital and a *school!*

Alongside the hospital or dispensary almost always stands a school or, more accurately, a chain of schools. In the Christian world mission as a whole, for every hospital or dispensary there are about twenty schools.

Again, a single illustration. Distinguished visitors to the United States from overseas frequently remark that America's most original and distinctive contribution to human culture has not been the skyscraper or Ford car or television or even the Negro spiritual; it has been—the woman's college. That contribution, American women through Christian missions have taken to the ends of the earth. All over the world one finds them—in Japan and Korea, in India and the Near East— the American woman's college transplanted, firmly rooted in foreign soil, now growing healthily there as an indigenous plant.

There is the Isabella Thoburn College at Lucknow in northern India, a monument to the vision, devotion, and generosity of American Methodist women, its spacious campus and beautiful, well-appointed buildings even more lovely than Wellesley or Vassar or Bryn Mawr. This is the historian's verdict: "Isabella Thoburn has pioneered most of the movements which now provide the dynamic for the new era for women in India. Its 'firsts' have been many—the first Indian woman college professor, Muslim doctor, professionally trained teachers, woman member of the Legislative Council." To that list was later added another "first." Isabella Thoburn's president, Miss Sarah Chakko, was not only a distinguished leader of free India; she was the first woman president, thus far the *only* woman president, of the World Council of Churches.

Thus, American womanhood has brought to the women of

the Orient emancipation, opportunity and training for leadership and, in consequence, priceless gifts to their nations.

But, once more, that is only a single and specialized illustration. There is no time to speak of the chain of magnificent Christian universities which stretch like jewels from Tokyo and Kyoto, through presently isolated China, and Calcutta and Bombay and all India, to Beirut and its American University (which Wendell Willkie, on his "one world" tour, discovered as the most impressive illustration of the "reservoir of good will" toward the United States, built up over the past century by Christian missions) and its sister institutions in Cairo, Istanbul, and elsewhere.

Behind these lies the whole vast enterprise of Christian primary and secondary education.

As I said earlier, a holiday in Nepal opened up to us *two* discoveries. First, the United Medical Mission with its multi-Protestant sponsorship. Alongside it and in the friendliest collaboration, a no less noteworthy Roman Catholic educational program. Everyone in Nepal from the king to the lowliest peasant knows Father Marshall O. Moran, S.J. And he knows more about Nepal than any other foreigner, an inexhaustible reservoir of information on its history, culture, religion. No wonder, for he has been in the country longer than any other outsider, having persuaded his way into Nepal, despite the legal ban on Christian evangelists, when it was first tentatively opened to visitors, and having been a universally respected and beloved figure in its life ever since. It was he who flew into the heart of the Himalayas to rescue Sir Edmund Hillery several years ago. He directs a chain of schools for boys and girls which parallel the Protestant hospitals and clinics.

I had determined not to visit India again without a

glimpse, however brief, of Travancore and its ancient Christian civilization. Here, in Kerala are two churches, the parent Syrian Orthodox or Jacobite Church and the "reformed" daughter, the Mar Thoma Church, which delight to claim their founding by the Apostle Thomas in the first century, which are testified by history to have been in strength on the Malabar coast by the fourth century, and which have continued their ancient faith and liturgy across more than 1,500 years in this land whose Christianity we tend to associate with the modern missionary outreach.

The moment one crosses into Kerala, he knows that he is in a "different India." He does not need to be told that the literacy rate of over 40 per cent is strikingly above that for India as a whole. As I was being driven to the airport for departure on a Monday morning, the car had to thread its way for more than an hour through streams of eager young boys and girls—books, slates, and notebooks crowding their arms as they hurried toward the Christian schools in determined quest of education. Nor does one need to be told that, despite the densest population in India, health conditions are extraordinarily good. Nor must one hear the oft-repeated Indian transposition of the threadbare Scots story— the story of the Scotsman who, on his return from a brief official mission to London, was asked by his wife whether he had met many interesting Englishmen and replied (with suitable Scots inflection), "Oh, no, Maggie; I was seeing only the heads of Departments!"—so universally recognized is the combination of tenacious regional loyalty and outstanding national leadership of citizens of Kerala.

I am bold to suggest that Kerala is the most authentic and convincing proving-ground of Christianity in Asia. For here is a church, or rather two related churches, rooted in the life and culture of the people centuries before our pagan and barbarian ancestors in northern Europe first left their tree-huts, learned of civilization or of Christian faith. Is it coincidence that the part of India where Christianity has flourished for over 1,500 years is also the area most advanced in education, health, and public service?

In Africa-south-of-the-Sahara-and-north-of-the-Transvaal until five years ago, 85 per cent of all education was still in mission schools. Today, in vast areas of Asia and Africa, especially among less advanced peoples, if there is to be any liberation of mind from total ignorance and tethering illiteracy, it will take place in Christian schools, and in Christian schools only.

We drove, mile after mile, hour after hour, along the dusty roads of Nigeria. One has the impression of only two types of buildings—native huts and Christian schools—every few miles, scores, hundreds of them, sponsored by a half dozen different denominations. Is it coincidence that Nigeria is the most promising of all the new African nations, perhaps the crucial testing ground of self-government in Africa?

Even where governments are beginning to rise to their responsibilities, Christian education still furnishes the indispensable foundations. In Ghana, in the first year of self-government, Kwame Nkrumah, then Prime Minister, and his colleagues quadrupled the budget for education and instituted universal primary education almost overnight. I asked the British Director of Education, who had stepped down from the post of Minister to take second place under a Ghanian, "Where in the world did you find teachers for three thousand new schools?" "Oh, from the missionary training college," he replied. "There is no other possible source." Nkrumah has given his testimony: like himself, every officer in his first government had been educated in Christian schools.

There was a day not so long ago in this country when medicine and education were services of the Christian Church; witness the names of many great city hospitals and the initial sponsorship of most American colleges, for example Harvard, "lest New England be cursed with an illiterate ministry." Throughout the world, the Christian Church is still the *pioneer* agency, often the *only* agency, for the healing of physical illness and emancipation from mental darkness. It is still teaching men and women and little children to worship the Lord their God with their whole strength and minds as well as with their hearts and souls. One may venture the judgment that that is the only truly sound basis of either education or medicine.

A hospital, a school, and a *church!*

The three major aspects of the Christian mission. But the order is climactic. What sends these doctors and nurses and teachers and agriculturists to the ends of the earth? What keeps them at their work, often in almost unendurable loneliness and in the face of well-nigh insupportable handicaps and discouragements? Behind all else, as its dynamic source and directing power, stands Christian faith and the church through which it is born, sustained, and transmitted.

Once again, space permits only a single illustration. It is drawn from that country which stands at the heart of the continent of Africa, a land of seemingly limitless undeveloped resources and pivotal strategic importance: the Congo. On neither of my trips to Africa was I able to see the veteran alumnus of Union Theological Seminary in the Congo. Ten years ago, his post was located three days by riverboat from

Leopoldville. My itinerary was too tight to permit the side trip. He was far too busy to take a week to come to see a representative of his Alma Mater. However, when I stopped briefly in Leopoldville, on the desk of the secretary of the American Baptist Mission I chanced to pick up the statistical report of his work for the previous year, written in clear, strong figures. Here they are:

1. His parish: an area roughly the size of Massachusetts
2. Its population: 140,000 Africans
3. Other denominations in this territory: none
4. Church membership: 7,763 *families,* 22,000 adults, an increase of 300 per cent during his five years of work
5. New members by adult baptism that year: 6,193
6. Local churches: 29, all entirely self-supporting
7. Other regular places of worship: 401
8. Church staff: 608 workers
9. Other ordained ministers: none
10. Budget for all church work: $17,000 a year
11. Schools under his supervision: 474. Pupils: 16,678. Teaching staff: 562
12. Contributions from African members for that year: $40,000, an increase of 40 per cent over the year before.

Statistics are cold facts, difficult for most of us to clothe with their human meanings. However, in terms of figures, what parish in the United States could equal that record— 22,000 members; staff of 1,100; increased giving in a single year, 40 per cent? What American minister could match that responsibility or that opportunity?

Chester and Margaret Jump have written letters home which have been gathered into a little booklet, *Congo Diary,* a fascinating journal crowded with humor and humanity, pathos and hard work, disheartenments and overflowing satisfactions. But through it all there runs an unintended refrain:

You see there is a great deal left undone. We haven't begun to mention all the things that could be done if we were quintuplets. But please don't think we are discouraged. In fact, perhaps we're in much too good a mood to write about the things we don't do because everything has gone well today.

But seriously, there is a burden in our hearts, a burden for the many thousands who don't know our Lord, for the many who are trying to follow His way but have so little help, who understand so imperfectly. The Lord has blessed us, and is continually helping us, but we need your prayers, we need your help, and we need some of you. There are too many tasks for two pairs of hands, but if we had even two pairs more, we could accomplish twice as much.

VI

This, then, is the overarching impression—the many-sided, rounded, comprehensiveness of the Christian world mission.

A second fact was made vivid for many at the World Council Assembly at New Delhi. Not a few of those who were there, including some with considerable previous ecumenical experience, testified that what struck them overwhelmingly was the discovery of *Christianity as a world reality.* As the "Message" declared: "Christianity now has a home in every part of the world."

Even a "plane's-eye view" of Christianity-around-the-world can hardly miss that fact. As one hops quickly from continent to continent and country to country, almost everything changes—climate, color of skin of the people, their clothes, customs, language, outlook. There is one thing, and almost only one thing, which is everywhere substantially the same: Christians and the Christian church—speaking varied tongues, to be sure, but the same language of belief and ideal; differing in race and history and background, but guided and united through allegiance to one Lord, one faith, one God and Father of all.

That suggests a final fact. The illustrations given above happen to have been drawn from the work of various denominations: Presbyterian medicine in Africa, Methodist and Syrian Orthodox education in India, Roman Catholic education in Nepal, Baptist evangelism in the Congo. They might as well have been taken from the work of a half dozen other Churches. Or they might all have been taken from the missions of a single Protestant denomination. Or, indeed, from Roman Catholic missions. For while there are important differences, the over-all programs of the two great branches of Christendom in their outreach across the world are strikingly parallel. For example, the most recent comprehensive statistics reported 55,122 Roman Catholic mission churches, and 55,395 Protestant mission churches, while the number of hospitals and dispensaries of the two movements was, by a strange coincidence, identical—3,433. And, although precise figures for their constituencies are not obtainable, they are roughly equal. This is the key fact: In the life and work of Christian missions, denominational differences count for almost nothing. It is the Christian world movement in its entirety, made up of countless individual centers and projects, sponsored by many different churches and missions, which is overwhelmingly impressive and important.

In the second century, an unknown Christian wrote to his friend Diognetus, "What the soul is in the body, that Christians are in the world. Christians hold the world together."

It may be that history's most important verdict upon these troubled times which are our fate will be: "Christianity held the world together."

VII

My colleagues and I, in these first four chapters, have sought to give you some impressions of Christianity on the march, through nineteen and a half centuries. Can any conclusions be drawn in summary? I shall suggest four; these are hardly more than paraphrases of the findings of our foremost historian of the "Expansion of Christianity," Dr. Kenneth Scott Latourette of Yale University in his monumental seven-volume "History" under that title.

The first stands forth on the record so unmistakably that he who runs may note. Through the years and down the centuries, the Christian Movement has swept forward in outreach across the earth's surface, in winning the allegiance of mankind and, so Dr. Latourette believes, in influence upon the common life of humanity.

No one can escape or deny that fact. A glance at a world map in successive epochs demonstrates that: from a tiny dot in a soon-to-die capital city near the eastern shore of the Mediterranean to every continent, every race, almost every people and tribe; from a handful of insignificant little companies meeting clandestinely in the back streets of Antioch and Jerusalem and Alexandria and Ephesus and Rome to unnumbered communities spread to the earth's ends, counting in their membership one-third of the human race; from obscure and despised ghettolike groups to a social force which challenges where it does not mold cultures and empires and civilizations, the mightiest corporate force in history.

Second, that advance has *not* been a steady, unbroken
progression, escalatorlike. On the contrary, it has been by a
sequence of alternate progress and decline—great forward
thrusts followed by sharp recessions. Dr. Latourette detects
four such massive epochs of march and retreat:

The first great advance carried the Christian Movement
in ever wider circles through close to five centuries, until
A.D. 500. Then came a catastrophic retreat, lasting 450 years
to A.D. 950, which wrested from Christian allegiance a full
half of the lands which, in 500, had been at least nominally
Christian—the severest setback Christianity has ever suffered.
However, there followed the first miracle of revival and recovery—a renewed thrust which carried Christianity far beyond its earlier utmost outreach and which persisted for four
hundred years, to about 1350. Again retreat set in, less severe
than before but devastating. The century and a half from
1350 to 1500 marked a period of relapse and loss. Once more,
recession was followed by still another and more extended
advance, which penetrated the western hemisphere and
touched Asia and the coasts of Africa, to about 1750. But
again the church faltered in strength and lost ground gravely,
from about 1750 to the early years of the last century. This
retreat was followed by the greatest outpouring of strength
in the whole of Christian history; the Christian Movement
reached peoples and power never equaled by any other force
in mankind's experience—the "Great Century" of which we
spoke earlier, using Dr. Latourette's phrase.

Third, each successive sweep of advance carried the reach
of the Christian Movement farther and the penetration of
Christian influence deeper than its prodecessor. Each successive retreat has been less severe and, to employ a military
metaphor, has been stabilized at a less rearward position than

its predecessor. Each recession has been succeeded by an even more wide-sweeping and far-reaching advance. Moreover, there has been an evident acceleration of pace in the alternate progress and decline, as is true of mankind's life as a whole.

Dr. Latourette dates the conclusion of the "Great Century" at 1914. The one overarching question-mark which shadows Christianity at this hour—the great unknown—is: Are we, then, on the threshold of, or perhaps already in, a period of recession?

We do not know. No one should assume retreat until it is proved. But there is no little evidence to support an affirmative answer to that question:

1. The constriction of Christianity in Russia, China, and other countries under Communist rule

2. The evident ill-health of churches in Great Britain and Europe generally

3. The problematic continuance and permanent results of the so-called "revival" in the United States

4. The precarious uncertainties for the youngest Christian churches in Africa-in-revolution

But there is a fourth and final lesson—perhaps the most important, as it is certainly the most unexpected—from this history of Christianity through nineteen centuries.

When recession overtakes the Christian Movement, it has almost always been most acute precisely where Christianity had seemed established in greatest strength, in the areas and at the centers of longest and deepest rootage. And, the obverse, Christianity has proved strongest to withstand the forces of disintegration and defeat, survival has been most vigorous, on the frontiers of the church's life, where its youth and vitality and its relative disengagement from a dying cul-

ture have enabled it to endure in strength. Even more striking
and more significant, when forward movement has been re-
sumed, as it always has, it has been empowered not from the
old historic centers of the church's existence but from these
youthful churches on its frontiers.

The lesson for us is clear. If we are entering, or are perhaps
already in, an epoch of retreat, we may confidently anticipate
that it will be succeeded in due time by another phase of
forward movement. And we know where to look for the
dynamic for recovery and renewed advance—to the youngest
churches of Asia and Africa, of Oceania and Latin America,
brought into existence during the "Great Century" by the
Christian world mission.

Are these youngest Christian churches adequate for so
demanding a role? There are few more important questions
for the future of Christianity. For many, the answer was pre-
saged at the World Council Assembly at New Delhi. Not a
few ecumenical veterans commented that this Assembly demonstrated that the Ecumenical Movement had "come of age."
There were others who discerned the most striking and surest
evidences of maturity, of coming of age, not in the World
Council as a whole but in one segment of its membership—the
Younger Churches. To be sure, there was no Younger Church
"bloc" comparable to the Asian–African bloc in the United
Nations. There was no distinctive Younger Church "theology." But there was a distinctive Younger Church voice,
though in many tongues. It spoke almost always with mature
confidence, realistic hopefulness, expectant optimism. In this
resonance, it sounded in sharp contrast to the prevailing,
more somber and hesitant, often doleful accents of Western
Older Churchmen. Doubtless, this is in part an echo of the
vigorous and buoyant expectation of the new nations, in

which so many Younger Churchmen are ardent participants. But it goes deeper than that. Within the past quarter-century, the leadership of the Younger Churches has achieved full independence and self-direction with resultant maturity. Within Christianity's world mission, there is a strong and confident outlook toward the future. The need now is that this attitude be reinfected in the leadership of the traditional churches of the west.

VIII

Lastly, how significant is this World Christian Movement today? It is important not to exaggerate its influence or to minimize its very considerable limitations.

In the first place, it embraces only a fraction of mankind—altogether, a large fraction, about one-third; but outside Europe and the Americas, only 3 to 5 per cent. And the movement for Christian unity includes only a part, about a third, of Christendom. The largest Christian Communion, the Church of Rome, takes no part in Ecumenical Christianity. And despite encouraging beginnings of "conversations" between Roman Catholic and Orthodox or Protestant churchmen, there is no realistic prospect of active participation by the Roman Church in Christian unity within the forseeable future.

However, this movement does embrace almost all principal Protestant bodies, an increasing number of Orthodox communions, such ancient Eastern churches as the Coptic, Ethiopian, Syrian, and others. In addition to the Church of Rome, only the churches in China, the Dutch Reformed Churches of South Africa, two large American Protestant bodies (Southern Baptist and Missouri Synod Lutheran), and the numerous—and rapidly multiplying—Pentecostal, Adventist, and Holiness groups hold aloof, remaining outside the ecumenical community. The Church of Christ in the world is more nearly one in fellowship and in organization for united witness and action than it has been since the schisms of the earliest centuries.

In the second place, this is still largely a movement of leaders of the Churches. It has hardly begun to take effective root in local communities. Ecumenical statesmen are agreed that the achievement of effective unity at the "grass roots," in local communities, is the major ecumenical imperative for the period immediately ahead.

However, this movement does claim the convinced and active allegiance of virtually all the foremost officers of its constituent churches. Most of them were present in person at New Delhi—the weightiest gathering of the leaders of Christendom who have ever assembled "with one accord, in one place" since the Day of Pentecost.

In the third place, the movement's influence upon the conflicts of nations has heretofore been limited by the separation of the "curtains" which divide the nations themselves. How far this limitation will be lifted through the adherence of the Church of Russia and its close affiliates cannot be forecast, for these Orthodox bodies have traditionally been chary of direct involvement in political and international issues. In any event, the most serious limitation upon the movement's effect upon world conflict is the churches' own conception of their role in public affairs. The Christian Church is not a political instrument to pit its strength against secular agencies and governments. The influences it disseminates and the manner of their working are too delicate, too subtle to register clearly in the crude calculus of empire.

Even here, however, that impact has been far greater than is generally known. Time and again, it has been proved that when the churches speak intelligently and act unitedly they are able to affect vitally the policies of nations and the decisions of statesmen. It was the insistence of the churches which was largely responsible for the transformation of the United Nations from the League of Great Powers which emerged from Dumbarton Oaks into the Assembly of all nations which was achieved at San Francisco, which forced the replacement of the old Mandates system by the Trusteeship principle, which led to the adoption of the Declaration of Human Rights and the formulation of a Charter of Rights. Since 1946, the two world Christian bodies united at New Delhi have jointly sponsored a Commission of the Churches on International Affairs with a modest but able and effective secretariat, known and respected by statesmen of all countries at the United Nations, whose representatives have helped to alleviate tension, prevent conflict, and effect constructive advance in some of the gravest crises of the past fifteen years. It was this fact which led John Foster Dulles to return to active participation in the work of the church. It was his own observation of the actual and weighty impact of the churches which prompted this judgment: "The Christian Church is a worldwide institution. . . . I know of my personal knowledge the profound influence that has been exerted upon Government by the public opinion that the Churches have created over recent years."

More ominous by far for the continuing advance of the world Christian movement than its own inherent limitations are forces which threaten it from outside: the inroad of Communistic atheism, which has greatly reduced the size while solidifying the strength of churches in Russia and China; in-

transigent nationalism in South Africa, which has led the
Dutch Reformed Churches there to withdraw from the World
Council; above all the imponderables and unpredictables for
Christianity implicit in the "African revolution."

IX

If it would be a mistake to exaggerate the Church's influence, it would be a no less grievous error to underestimate its
significance.

The world-wide movement of the Christian Church!

There is nothing else like it in the world. There has been
nothing else like it in the whole of human history. The truth is
that there is nothing which can so much as be compared
with it. No other movement has ever spread so rapidly and
widely in so brief a period of time. No other allegiance holds
today, or has ever held, the loyalty of so large a number and
proportion of the human race—about one-third of mankind,
as we have seen earlier. There is no other movement or organization (if we except world Communism) which reaches
into every race and nation and people, overpassing every
barrier which otherwise sunders them; no other which binds
them in a living spiritual community.

It would be an exaggeration to say that the only rays of
light piercing the gloom of our world's present outlook come
from the Christian Movement. It would be an overstatement
of the truth. The truth is: There is no other force spread
widely through our contemporary world and disseminating
through the whole body of humanity influences for the right-
ing of its wrongs, the healing of its deepest maladies, the
bridging of its divisions, possibly even the halting of its fatal-
istic descent toward conflict and chaos. There is no other

agency reaching out toward every corner of the earth, toward every people and every aspect of human life—for health and enlightenment, for reconciliation and redemption. There is no other institution or movement which still holds together the shattered fragments of humanity, as an earnest to all men of what God intended the life of mankind to be and what some day the family of nations may become.

With all its divisions, its inadequacies, its apostasies, the world Christian movement is today the greatest power for the uplifting of the life of humanity in its every aspect and for the building of a fairer world that this planet has ever seen. Its powerful advance, with incalculable benefit to mankind, waits upon our realization of that fact; for it is a fact. And then upon our appropriate response to that fact.

PART III

CHRISTIANITY AND ITS
MAJOR CONTEMPORARY RIVALS

5. Christianity and Its Major Rivals in Asia

RAJAH BHUSHANAM MANIKAM

The subject of Part III is "Christianity and Its Major Contemporary Rivals." I have been asked to write particularly on rivals to Christianity in the part of the world from which I come, but I dare say that those rivals are to a certain extent influencing life in other parts of the world also.

I come from East Asia. It is important at the very beginning to say a few words about the present situation in East Asia, bearing upon these challenges to Christianity. If you fly from Karachi, Pakistan, to Seoul in Korea, Tokyo in Japan, Manila in the Philippines, Colombo in Ceylon, and then go back to Karachi, you will have covered one-twentieth of the world's area, and in this one-twentieth of the world's area lives one-half of mankind. The other nineteen-twentieths of the world houses the rest of mankind. So, what affects life and conditions in that part of the world affects one-half of mankind, and that must necessarily have some meaning for the other half as well.

It is in this region that Christianity must come to grips with the major classical, ancient religions of the world: Hinduism, Buddhism, Islam, Shinto, Confucianism, and so forth. It is not in America that Christianity has to come to grips with these religions, but it is in that part of the world, and only there, that Christianity must meet the challenges of these religions that are becoming resurgent.

I have chosen three major rivals to Christianity from the religious field, and two rivals from the ideological field.

I

From the religious field I would like to present the challenges that come from the revival of three great religions of the world: Hinduism, Islam, and Buddhism. I remember in my student days the slogan of the Student Volunteer Movement: "Win the world in this generation for Christ." No longer do we hear such a slogan. These religions, instead of dying out, have become revitalized and are contending against the exclusive claims of Christianity. Therefore, those who belong to the Christian faith have to understand the challenges that come to it from these revived, resurgent religions.

Let me begin with *Hinduism*.

Who is a Hindu? The only definition that one can attempt to give is that a Hindu is a person who is born in the Hindu faith, in a Hindu family, and who has not openly renounced the Hindu faith. This may sound strange, but it contains a good deal of truth. Hinduism, unlike Islam or Buddhism or Christianity, has no creed, no confession, no founder. It is a way of life. It is indeed old, coming from the dim ages of the past, adding to itself many things as it lived through the

ROMAN EMPIRE—THE STATE
MYSTERY RELS—MITHRAISM
ISLAM—TOURS

world—many accretions, many elements of value from other religions. Today, purified and reformed, it is challenging the exclusive claims of Christianity.

There are in the world today roughly 285,000,000 Hindus, ✗ a very large number indeed. The majority live in my country of India. To be sure, you will see Hinduism practiced by emigrants from India to other parts of the world. You will find Hindu swamis and yogis even in America. The whole of Indonesia was under its sway until Islam came to Indonesia and drove Hinduism out. Now, all that is left of Hinduism in Indonesia is to be seen largely in Javanese life, dances, and music, and in that beautiful island of Bali.

What is Hinduism? And what is its challenge to Christianity? Hinduism is very eclectic. It has all kinds of religious beliefs. It has animism for those primitive people who would believe it and derive something from it. It has popular polytheism, many gods, and those who would like to believe in those gods may do so. It has pietistic theism with a personal god, and philosophic monism, which is largely ideological. It also has agnostic mysticism by which the believer becomes one with God, and then the distinction between oneself and God does not exist. So, you see, Hinduism is a very eclectic, flexible something in which anybody in any stage of life can find his own satisfaction and inspiration for life.

Nevertheless, there are four basic assumptions in Hinduism today which make a tremendous appeal to the peoples of the West, even to Christians. The first assumption is that there is an ultimate reality. It is a fact that ultimately there is *one* reality; call it what you will—Brahma, God, Buddha—whatever term you give it, that ultimate reality exists. It cannot be fully comprehended by the finite mind of man. He can know something about this ultimate reality, but being man, being finite, he cannot fully comprehend the infinite. Thus, we can have only partial manifestations of the full truth.

The second main assumption follows from the first. If ultimate reality exists and cannot be comprehended, then no theological formulation of it is at all possible. All religions are only attempts at knowing God, they can never know him fully. And so religions are partial manifestations of the ultimate reality. No religion can ever dare call itself final, or claim final validity. It is here that Hinduism challenges the final validity and the exclusive claims of Christianity. We can have only interpretations of that ultimate reality, and, therefore, let us be tolerant of each other. Let no religion fight another religion because, at best, even the purest of religions is but a partial manifestation of godhead. Tolerance is the key word, not bigotry, not religious imperialism (to force another person to believe as you believe), but sympathetic understanding of the other man's belief and tolerance of him.

The third basic assumption is that all religions are alike in the sense that they are only partially true. This point is important because often Western critics condemn Eastern philosophers when they say that all religions are alike. Men like Radhakrishnan and others have enough sense to know that religions teach different things and they do not, therefore, claim identical equality in every respect amongst the religions. But the main point that is made, and very often misunderstood, is this: that all religions are alike in that they are only partial manifestations of the truth. Therefore we cannot think in terms of one religion alone being superior to other religions. The sum total of all religions will be better than any one religion. This teaching has led to a great deal of syncretism and, all the way through, the Hindu mind is syncretic. When Buddhism comes and fights against Hinduism, Hinduism absorbs it, makes Buddha one of the *avatars,* one of the incarnations, and drives Buddhism out of India. It has a tremendous absorbing power, and it is attempting to do the same with Christianity today. It wants to make Jesus Christ one of the *avatars,* one of the incarnations, and thereby absorb him in the pantheon of gods.

Lastly, the Hindus say that whatever one's religious beliefs may be (and one has a perfect right to choose any religious belief he wants), that person must realize that his belief is not the fullest truth. The main thing is to adopt the Hindu way of life, the Hindu *dharma,* the deeds and the life that the Hindu should do and live, that which is most useful. And so Hinduism becomes a strongly pragmatic religion.

Every religion in the world has three aspects. There is first the *creed;* then there is the *cultus;* finally there is the *culture* —the creed, the cultus, and the culture.

The *creed* is what one believes, what the religion teaches, the confession of a religion. In that respect Hinduism has the main assumptions but has no definite creed like the Apostles Creed or the Nicene Creed.

Second, it has a *cultus*—the rites, the rituals, the forms of worship; and it is here that Hinduism is trying to reform itself today. It is not becoming more and more polytheistic; it is becoming more and more theistic. When Mahatma Gandhi sat down and worshiped, and sang, *"Ram, ram, sita ram,"* it was a personal deity that he was thinking of. Hinduism today in its cultus is giving up a great deal of idol worship. Idol worship is all right for the man who wants something to help him think of God. Even the primitive Hindu will be able to have something that will draw him to the thought of God. But the Hindu who is educated (and spiritually does not need these helps, these images, these idols) leaves these idols behind. Idol worship is gradually disappearing. Temples are being thrown open to outcastes. Until recently no outcaste man was allowed to enter a Hindu temple to worship therein, and many Christian missionaries have criticized this. Hinduism has been quickened in its conscience and now all temples are by law open both to the highcaste and to the outcaste. Many cultus reforms have been effected.

Third, the *culture*. The religious culture of the people, the literature that is being produced largely to commend Hinduism to the people of India, is being emphasized. It is religious literature, music, thought forms, life forms, forms of living, revival of music, revival of dance, revival of ancient literature. All these things are in the cultural realm, and again there are many reforms. The main thing to note is this: While these reforms are taking place in the outer spheres, at the very heart of Hinduism, at the inner core, its creed, there is not much change. In cultus, yes, there is much change. In culture there is much change. The Hindu *view* of life may be changed, but the Hindu *way* of life must not change. And there is a vast difference between the two. So, in its inner core there has not been very much change, and Hinduism persists in living through the centuries in more or less the same way.

The man who has done most to popularize Hinduism is the president of India, Radhakrishnan, the philosopher. We could call him the "philosopher king" of Plato's *Republic*. He was, by profession, a teacher of philosophy and now he is the president of India. For a long time he held a chair of Eastern religions at Oxford University, and he has written many, many books, and commended Hinduism to the people of the world.

There are three main emphases that Radhakrishnan is making at the present time. The first is that man is not an absolute by himself. Man finds the fullest satisfaction in God, and man is man only when he becomes conscious of God and lives a life of fellowship with him in such a way that the distinction "I" and "Thou" no longer exists. *"Tut tum asi*—Thou art one with Him." So, man has no existence of his own, but has to live in God; though he cannot fully comprehend God, he can at least know something of him, and man is man only when he grows into that fellowship with God, when distinctions between man and God cease, and the two become one.

Second, it follows from the above that it is necessary to work out a world community. We talk about the United Nations and a world community, and here is a Hindu philosopher who has been stressing this in his writings for many years. The Greek and Roman world emphasized rationality. The Hebrew–Christian world emphasized a personal deity. The Hindu world does not emphasize rationality, because with the mind one cannot apprehend God, not even a personal god, because one can never know whether God is a person. You think that God is a person only because you are a person. So, the Hindu world emphasizes that there is an in-dwelling God, a God that dwells in man. Discover that God, and have a world community of all those who discover him also. Therefore, all religions must co-operate and not fight with one another. All religions are imperfect anyhow. A perfect religion is yet to be. So, why talk about the finality of any religion? Why do not religions, instead of fighting with each other, work together to establish this world community?

The third important point that Radhakrishnan has brought out in his writings is the tremendous appeal that he makes, which I call "missionary appeal," namely, respect for all religions. Again and again he stresses that that is the mark of a cultured person, one who has respect for religions and not an intolerance or bigotry toward them. When a great conference of world religions met in New Delhi recently, Radhakrishnan spoke these words at that meeting: "If this conference makes you respectful towards other religions and other human beings and makes you feel that there are no chosen races, no chosen nations, no chosen individuals, but each one has in him the possibility of growing with the Divine, this conference would have done well and achieved something." There you see the whole trend against a chosen people, revealed religion, perfect religion, and the like. There are many people, even in the United States of America, who are attracted by this kind of religious philosophy, namely, respect for other religions. All religions have had many accretions, and these accretions must be eliminated. Then, one finally arrives at that world community in which religions, instead of trying to supplant each other, will begin to supplement each other.

I pass on now to the second great religious rival of Christianity, which is *Islam*.

There are today 375,000,000 people who believe in Islam. There is a solid block extending from Turkey to Pakistan, with Indonesia on the other side and India between. Islam is no foreign religion to Christian people. We have only to think of the Crusades and all the bloody wars that Christians fought against Islam. Islam sprang up at a time when the Arabian world had greatly degenerated and worshiped 365 idols, one idol per day. Naturally, when Muhammad rose up he was bitter against idolatry, and the Muslim today is known for his fervor in breaking idols. All through the struggle between Islam and Hinduism in India, the Muslim has always been breaking idols, whereas the Hindu has been creating idols.

One can understand the reason behind this strong opposition to idolatry. Muhammad, as it is said, had many revelations given to him by St. Gabriel and he preached these revelations as truth. These truths were recorded by his disciple Abu Bakr, among others, and the recorded book is the Quran, the sacred book of the Muslims. The word "Islam" means "submission to God—not my will but Thy will be done" and Islam means submission to the commands of Allah.

There are five main duties that every Muslim has to perform:

First, he must believe there is no God but Allah, and Muhammad is his prophet. No God but Allah—not a trinitarian conception of God at all. It is one of the things that we as Christians in trying to propagate our religion among Muslims are faced with, an absolutely unitarian concept of God that has nothing to do with the trinitarian concept. There is no God but Allah, and after all, Muhammad is but his prophet, not God.

Second, the Muslim must pray five times a day. Sometimes he puts the Christian to shame. I have traveled in Indian trains in a second-class compartment with a number of Muslims and at six o'clock in the evening, wherever the train might be, any Muslim in the compartment would take out his prayer carpet, put it down, kneel, turn his face to Mecca, and pray. He cared not whether others looked at him or laughed. The Muslim is not ashamed of his religion. He must pray, pray with his face toward Mecca, five times daily.

The third duty of every Muslim is to give alms—charity. Muslims the world over are famous for their hospitality. Once you have eaten salt in a Muslim's house, you can never be murdered by him!

The fourth main thing that the Muslim must do is to fast through the month of Ramadhan, fasting all during the day. Not one morsel of food should go into him, although exceptions are permitted for reasons of health. Then in the evening, after a prayer, he may break his fast. One month of fasting and prayer is enjoined upon all Muslims.

And lastly, every Muslim must, if possible, make at least one pilgrimage to the sacred city of Mecca.

These are the five great duties that have been enjoined upon the Muslims.

There are today two main sects: the Sunnis, who believe in selecting their caliph by democratic means, and the Shias, whose caliphs succeed to power by hereditary claims.

Two forms of Islam are prevalent in the world today. One is Sufism, which is mystical Islam, and the other is Bahaism, and there are Bahai temples even in the United States.

Islam makes no distinction between church and state. To talk about a separation of the two is wrong, as the two are one. Pakistan is an Islamic state. There is no state church; there is only a church state. The two are one.

What is the great attraction of Islam to the people of the world? Its great simplicity of faith. No theological speculation, as in the Hindu or Christian religions, just very simple duties that a man should carry out and by which he should live: worship one God, give alms, pray, fast, if possible go to Mecca—a religion of simplicity. Drink is prohibited. If anybody touches alcohol, he is not a true Muslim. If anybody would bow down to wood and stone, he cannot be a Muslim.

The second great thing about the appeal of Islam and its challenge to Christianity is that there is only one God and that is Allah—no idols, no intermediaries, no other persons in one godhead, but one God.

The most important appeal, the third one, that Islam makes to all the world today is its stress upon brotherhood. I want to say to you that of all the religions I know, the one religion that not only professes brotherhood but practices it is Islam. I wish I could say this of Christianity, but that would not be true. In Islam you have an absolute brotherhood, and the Muslims are proud of this fact. This is one of the reasons why today Islam is spreading faster in Africa than the Christian religion is. Therefore, its challenges are powerful to the professions of Christianity, which preaches a brotherhood of man under a fatherhood of God but seldom practices it.

I turn now to Christianity's third great religious rival, *Buddhism,* which has spread all over the world.

Buddha was a Hindu prince from a first-class Indian home. He grew up there and saw terrible sights of suffering. He saw a man diseased. He saw an old man, age creeping up on him. He saw a dead man. And he saw a man who had renounced the world, a monk. These four sights worried him. He was born in a princely home. He knew no suffering, and here was a diseased man, here was a dead man, here was an old man, here was a man who had given up every material thing in life. Perhaps that last man, the monk, was really the happiest man. And so, Buddha began to renounce the world, to pursue something that would give him absolute peace of mind. Then came the great enlightenment under the Bo tree: "From good comes good; from evil comes evil." Thus, there is no use for idols. There is no use for sacred books. There is no use for cults. And so he preached his great religion to the people.

The fundamental thesis of Buddhism is this: All existence involves suffering. If you are a man, you are born to suffer.

All suffering comes by desires which are unfulfilled. We desire this and we desire that and when our desires cannot be fulfilled we suffer. My next door neighbor has a Cadillac and I have only a Ford, so I must acquire something better than a Cadillac to be better than my neighbor. When I cannot get it and my desire is not fulfilled, I suffer. All suffering is due to desire, and all sufferings will cease only when man does not go about selfishly desiring this and that for himself. When you can put away your desires, then you will arrive at a great state of mind called *Nirvana*, the state of perfect peace of mind unassailed by desires. Therefore, it is useless to go on pilgrimages, to mortify the body, or to believe in caste.

Buddhism started within Hinduism as a protest movement against caste. A man does not become a Brahman because he is born into a Brahman family. In whom there is truth and righteousness, he is a Brahman.

Buddha said, "My doctrine knows no distinction between high and low, rich and poor. It is like the sky—it has room for all. It is like water that washes all."

Once Buddha had a conversation with a woman who was drawing water from the well. This is a parallel to our Lord's conversation with the Samaritan woman. He asked her for water, and she said, "I am an outcaste. How could I give you water?" Then he said to her, "My sister, I did not ask thee for your caste or family. I beg water of thee if thou can give it to me. To him in whom love dwells, the whole world is but one family."

So he preached the brotherhood that knows no caste distinctions.

He said that God cannot be comprehended, and, therefore, why worry about Brahma, what his attributes are, whether he is a *Nigurna* Brahma, a Brahma without qualifications.

That is all idle speculation. Do not worry about it. Follow the eightfold path of Buddhism.

What is the eightfold path of Buddhism? Right belief, right resolve, right speech, right behavior, right occupation, right effort, right contemplation, and right concentration. Belief, resolve, speech, behavior, occupation, effort, contemplation, and concentration. And if one follows this eightfold path, one will have happiness in life.

There are two great divisions in Buddhism today. One, northern Buddhism, is called Mahayana Buddhism. You find it in Formosa, to a certain extent in Singapore and Malaya, in China, in Korea, in Japan, and so forth. This Buddhism has deified Buddha. It believes in prayer to him. It worships Buddha, though he was one who denied Godhead, at least to the extent that he did not know whether Brahma existed since one cannot know him. Yet Buddha himself became a deity and is worshiped in Mahayana Buddhism.

Then there is southern Buddhism, found in Thailand, in Malaya, in Burma, and in Ceylon. It is called the Hinayana Buddhism. There is no deification of Buddha in this form of Buddhism, but Hinduism exercises a great deal of the influence because of India, which is close to Ceylon.

What is the great challenge to Christianity that comes from Buddhism? There are three great challenges today. One is that Buddhism challenges activistic Christianity. From morning until evening we do this and we do that. We exist, but we do not live. And Buddhism says, "Why not become contemplative? Why not take time to meditate?" A great many meditation centers have been opened by Buddhists in places like Vipathanas and Lokiasamitas, where all kinds of physical practices are being indulged in. Christians are challenged to come and see whether in these ways they too cannot have a meditative life. The Buddhist says to the Christian, "You don't know anything about this? Why don't you come and get a mastery of yourself in these centers—not only a mastery of yourself, but acquire some supernatural power that will come to you through these exercises and through meditation?" Thus activistic Christianity is being challenged.

In the second place, Buddhism claims to be a rational religion. In Buddhism there are no superstitions, no philosophical systems of thought. Many scientists praise Buddhism today. While Christianity is being attacked as a religion with many unscientific assumptions and unwarranted theological dogmas, Buddhism is praised as a simple, rational religion with no superstitions.

The third challenge that Buddhism presents to Christianity today is that Buddhism is the one hope of bringing peace into the world. U Nu, the prime minister of Burma, once asked me, "What is the use of Christians getting together in a World Council of Churches and going to Evanston in 1954 to study about Christ being the hope of the world? How can Christ be the hope of the world when the nations which have been practicing his precepts for so many centuries have fought two bloody wars and are itching for a third? The only thing that can bring peace into the world is Buddhism of good will, of peace." And, he added, "Have I not built, right outside Rangoon, the Buddhist Pagoda? And if you go there, you will see that the Buddhist Pagoda stands for peace. It is a peace pagoda."

So, the Buddhists are one with all the people in the world who are longing for peace and are saying that the way of peace is more through Buddhism than through Christianity.

II

I go on now to two ideologies that are contending for the heart and soul of man today. Asia has been regarded as an ideological battleground. There are five main ideologies: Liberal Democracy (and democracy has become a religion with many people); Socialism (another great ideological rival to Christianity); Religious Nationalism—and very powerful at the present time; Gandhism, the whole philosophy of Gandhi; and Communism, which is spreading faster in Asia than any religion I know.

I shall deal very briefly and sketchily with only two of these: Religious Nationalism and Communism.

Today Asia is being swept by nationalism. Nationalisms have developed in a peculiar way. The nationalisms of the West grew because of rivalry and fighting between the countries. Germany fought France and that gave rise to a German nationalism and a French nationalism. But Asian nationalism did not come that way, not Asian countries fighting amongst ourselves, but fighting imperialism, fighting colonialism. Thus the Asian nations became nationalistic. This is still going on at a tremendous pace at the present time.

This nationalism is not entirely political, but has taken a religious coloring; that is the most terrible thing about Asian nationalism today. This Religious Nationalism says that the religions of the land should be revived, purified, and followed. Therefore, why take on an alien religion like Christianity? Shinto is enough for Japan, as is Buddhism for Thailand and Burma, Islam for Pakistan and Indonesia, and Hinduism for India. Revive your national culture, which is a religious culture, and make your religion the important dynamic of your life.

So, Religious Nationalism has been spreading. If you would be a 100 per cent Pakistani in Pakistan today, you cannot be a Christian Pakistani, nor a Hindu Pakistani, but you must be a Muslim Pakistani. In other words, to be a Pakistani 100 per cent, you have to belong to the religion of Islam. If you are going to be a Burman, a 100 per cent citizen of Burma, you cannot be a Christian Burman, nor a Hindu Burman, but you must be a Buddhist Burman. Thus Asian nationalism has become strongly religious.

I remember talking to a Thai girl in Bangkok about religion and the appeal and challenge of Christianity. She said to me, "Why should I accept this foreign religion? My king is the defender of my faith. And so, why should I not keep my religion, and revive that religion—take away the accretions from my religion and hold on to what is true within it?"

This attitude has a tremendous appeal, and also many dangers. The one great danger is that it has become a disruptive force and is breaking out in violence. You see religious groups claiming themselves to be the 100 per cent citizens of the land, and all other religious minorities are said to be foreigners in their own land, and thus rivalries and conflicts arise between these communities.

The second great drawback of Religious Nationalism is that it has no economic or social program. It only talks of religious matters and forgets that man is not just soul, but is also body and mind. It has no economic and no social program. Such a Religious Nationalism cannot today build a better Asia.

A third danger results from the fact that religious minorities are likely to be downtrodden if they cannot have the same rights and privileges as the majority religion. Religious Nationalism, therefore, instead of unifying a country, divides it into religious groups. Pakistan itself came into being on the basis of a people believing in a particular religion—not geography but culture and religion, unifying a people and making them a nation. For the first time in the world's history, a nation was born on the basis of religion.

I want to close this chapter with the second ideology, the appeal and challenge of Communism. I have already indicated that this is spreading very fast, making unparalleled progress in Asia. Where is Communism in power in East Asia today? It is in China, in North Korea, in North Vietnam, and in Kerala, one of the provinces or states of India. Where is Communism in conflict? In Korea, Burma, Malaya, and the Philippines. Where is it a legal party as long as it obeys the government established by law and order? In India, Ceylon, Burma, Indonesia, Pakistan, and Japan.

What is the appeal of Communism to the peoples of Asia? How does it challenge the claims of Christianity? There are four powerful appeals issuing from Communism, and we ought to understand these before we condemn Communism.

One is its great appeal for economic and social justice. Remember, you are dealing in Asia with people in great poverty, want, and hunger. The distinction between the rich and the poor is very great. Those who are rich are fabulously rich, and those who are poor are despicably poor. It must not be forgotten that there are some rich people in Asia. The richest man in the world is supposed to be an Indian. But along with these rich people, there are also the poor, and they are in a large majority. Communism comes along and speaks of what Russian has been able to do in the last fifty years, what China is doing today, and says that capitalism will never give economic and social justice. Many do not know of the benevolent capitalism in the United States of America, but know only of the capitalism which is a selfish capitalism, wherein the rich man continues to make large amounts of money. Communism hold a tremendous appeal for the poor, urging them to accept the Communist way of life and the Communist ideology.

The second great appeal of Communism to Asian groups is its stress on racial equality. It says that the Asian today has been condemned. He is not even called an Asian, but an Asiatic. We do not speak about a Europeatic; we speak about a European. We do not speak about an Americatic; we speak only of Americans. But the poor Asian is always an Asiatic. There is something of a sting to it. And the peoples of Asia and Africa believe that they will never get racial equality as things are going today. They are asked to look at Russia and what its ethnic minorities are enjoying in that country, supposedly. That kind of philosophy and propaganda makes a tremendous appeal to the peoples who are not today being recognized as racial equals in the world.

The third great appeal that Communism makes is for the political independence of a nation. How relevant and appealing this is to the peoples of Asia who have been ruled by many different European powers for centuries! Colonialism, even today, is not dead in Asia. Imperialism is fighting with its last breath, but it is still holding on. So, Communism comes along as a great supporter of the oppressed peoples and makes a tremendous appeal.

In the fourth place, there is a religious appeal also. It is almost a parody to talk about Communism, which does not profess belief in a God, making a religious appeal and yet it is fast becoming a substitute faith. Many today who have no more faith in a religion find in Communism all the vigor and fervor of a religion—a philosophy of life, a program of action, an object of devotion. The Communists have a clear-cut program. They know where they are going. Many of us drift, drift, and drift. They have a clear-cut ideology, and therefore Communism has a religious appeal for these persons.

However, there are some factors which are working against Communism in Asia. One is the opposition of nationalism to world-wide Communism. Communists are being suspected of being more pro-Russian than pro-Indian or pro-Japanese or pro-Burmese. The Comminform is a world group, and therefore Religious Nationalism comes into violent conflict with Communism. In the second place, there is a tremendous dislike of the violence that goes along with the Communistic program of action. In the third place, there is a great antipathy to the atheistic teachings of Communism. After all is said and done, the Asian is incorrigibly religious. And so, being a religious man, he does not have much use for an irreligious philosophy of life.

Lastly (and this is very important and often forgotten), there is a great disillusionment with Communist propaganda and promises. That in itself is acting against Communism. Hungary is not forgotten; it is known all over Asia. When Communism talks about political independence, we know something about the Communist satellites and what amount of freedom they have. Therefore, there is a large amount of disillusionment in the Communist prophecies and promises. But nobody knows how long these factors are going to fight Communism successfully.

Two experiments are going on in Asia—one in China on the Communist way of life, and one in my own country, India, on an entirely democratic, parliamentary system of government. The rest of Asia is looking at these two experiments.

If the Indian experiment succeeds, then there is hope that the rest of Asia will not go Communist.

I went to end by pointing out that the best way to combat this ideology of Communism is not military pacts, SEATO and NATO, and military bases. You cannot put down an ideology with might. You can, however, drive out one idea by a better idea. You can torture a man, but the idea will be with him until he breathes his last. A better ideology must be brought into the fight against Communism.

As a convinced Christian, I know of no better alternative to Communism than for Christians—all Christians—to practice what we profess as Christians. Let us give unto our fellow man political independence, and live that fullest and abundant life, for Jesus Christ came that we may have life and have it more abundantly.

6. Christianity and
Secularist Humanism

JOHN C. BENNETT

Labels are usually inaccurate or misleading. This chapter is about trends in the intellectual and spiritual life in our time which are real. The label "Secularist Humanism" chosen to suggest them is a dubious one. Although Stoic Existentialism and Secularist Humanism may overlap, there is a clear difference. Many of the "modern Stoics" of Chapter 7 of this book could also be classified as Secularist Humanists, but they are a special kind; they are those who have become preoccupied with the anxieties and frustrations of life, with man's finiteness and death. They may also join with the Secularist Humanists of this Chapter in the support of many of the same causes. Albert Camus was a prime example of this. Jean-Paul Sartre for some years combined his existentialist form of modern Stoicism with the political support of Communism. This was surprising in view of his devotion to an absolute and unstructured freedom.

We are not dealing here with as interesting individuals as

the modern Stoics but with the almost unconscious everyday faith of most conscientious people in our time (your next door neighbor is not likely to be a modern Stoic, but it is quite likely that he may be a Secularist Humanist). Few of the people who belong to this general category are as enthusiastic or as confident about the objects of their faith or the goals of their lives as was the case with men of similar faith or goals from about 1750 to 1925, and yet what I am calling Secularist Humanism is still the chief rival of Christianity in the Western world. And there is no more intelligent or nobler representative of it than the Prime Minister of India.

Now a few words about the label itself: Secularist Humanism. "Humanism" is a great word that refers to philosophies of life which stress the specifically human both against the subhuman and against the kind of emphasis on the superhuman that devaluates the human. It was used by the school of literary humanists of a generation ago represented by Irving Babbitt and Paul Elmer More to describe a protest against some of the very things which I am calling humanism. They protested against the democratic humanitarianism which seemed to them to level down the peaks of human excellence in the interests of equality. They feared that the discriminations of the intelligence were being swamped by emotion. They did not necessarily reject Christianity, but they insisted on a form of Christianity which was consistent with their high view of the human. Indeed, there have been Christian humanists in most periods.

This general "humanism" has kinship with the classical humanism of Plato and Aristotle. But at the same time there is a kind of humanism which gives less attention to the peaks of excellence and more attention to the broader possibilities of humanity, that rejects faith in God as transcending man,

A. EUSTACE HAYDON   M. C. OTTO
J. A. C. F. AUER   R. W. SELLARS

that hopes to mobilize all the resources of science in the sense of experimental intelligence for the realization of these human possibilities.

I have used the word "secularist" to suggest the fact that this humanistic faith has cut itself loose from the Christian tradition. There may be some arbitrariness in this use of words. But I should distinguish here between "secular" and "secularist." When we speak of the secular, we merely refer to the fact that there are areas of human interest and activity which are not under the direct guidance of religious authorities or of theology as an intellectual discipline. The church and theology should allow these interests and activities to develop according to their inner logic. We have to be careful here because I do not mean that there is any human interest which is separate from the purpose of God or that there is any human interest which may not have effects on our lives that come within the area of the concern of the church. But the church should allow science and art and many aspects of politics and economics to develop freely and not seek to control them from without. Christians working in these areas will think and act as Christians and they will bring Christian motives and sensitivities to what they do, but these Christians will work within the interests and activities themselves insofar as we thnk of them as secular. The secular is not in itself opposed to Christian faith. It is to be welcomed as a part of the goodness of God's creation. To accept the secular may often be a form of emancipation for the human mind.

"Secularist," on the other hand, is a word that refers to a philosophy of life which asserts itself over against Christian faith. It seeks to organize life as though God did not exist. Secularist or secularism is thus to be contrasted with the secular. When I put together the words "Secularist Humanism"

I am merely trying to suggest that there is a pervasive trend which rejects the claims of Christianity and which still maintains a morally sensitive concern for high human values and goals. Two American books express this trend from two different generations but from the same Columbia University: John Dewey's *A Common Faith* and Charles Frankel's *The Case for Modern Man*. Sir Julian Huxley is one of the most illustrious Secularist Humanists.

At the end of Chapter 7, Tom F. Driver refers to the fact that Western man has "come of age." That expression is emphasized by Dietrich Bonhoeffer in his letters from prison entitled *Prisoner for God* and it suggests something that the modern Stoics and Communists and the Secularist Humanists have in common. Bonhoeffer describes this situation of having "come of age" in the following passage:

The movement beginning about the thirteenth century—towards the autonomy of man (under which head I place the discovery of the laws by which the world lives and manages in science, social and political affairs, art, ethics and religion)—has in our time reached a certain completion. Man has learned to cope with all questions of importance without recourse to God as a working hypothesis. In questions concerning science, art and even ethics, this has become an understood thing which one scarcely dares to tilt at any more. But for the last hundred years or so it has become increasingly true of religious questions also: it is becoming evident that everything gets along without God, just as well as before. As in the scientific field, so in human affairs generally, what we call "God" is being more and more edged out of life, losing more and more ground.[1]

This process that Bonhoeffer describes has gone further in an explicit way in Europe than in America. There remains

here a combination of a general religiousness with real defer-
ence to the Christian tradition and the churches (including
Jewish traditions and synagogues) which is surprising to
many Europeans. They would probably regard our revival of
interest in religion as the last gasp of something which is
basically irrelevant in our world. Bonhoeffer might or might
not have agreed with that, but even if he had, he would have
said that there is a revelation of God in Christ which is not to
be identified with religion or even with Christianity and that
Christ may transform this modern mind. Bonhoeffer's death
as one of the true Christian martyrs deprived the church of a
thinker who was beginning to deal in a radically new way
with this problem. He has left us only hints of what he might
have come to say to us. But even these hints have made him
one of the commanding figures in contemporary theology.

Let me put beside that passage from the German theologian Bonhoeffer the following passage from Dr. Corliss
Lamont's *Humanism as a Philosophy*. Dr. Lamont is one of
the most articulate humanists and one of those most dedicated to high humane values. He writes:

It is evident, then, that God, once imagined to be an omni-
present force throughout the whole world of Nature and man,
has been increasingly tending to seem omniabsent. Everywhere
intelligent and educated people rely more and more on purely
secular and scientific techniques for the solution of their problems. As science advances, the belief in divine miracle and the
efficacy of prayer becomes fainter and fainter. Certain popular
sayings have long recognized this situation, such as Benjamin
Franklin's "God helps those who help themselves" and the more
recent "Praise the Lord and pass the ammunition." Today the
prevailing tendency in a culturally advanced country like America, regardless of what formal tributes may be paid to traditional

faiths, is to retire the Almighty from his former role in this-earthly affairs and to look upon him as a sort of Honorary Chairman of the Universe.[2]

This general trend which combines rejection of the claims of any historic religious faith with a high-minded and sensitive concern for humane values has been institutionalized in various ways, which many of you will recognize as I mention them. This outlook has often been the dominant one in universities and especially in departments of philosophy, psychology, and the social sciences. It has been highly influential in schools of education. It has often characterized professional social work. Today there are trends which move in another direction, which at least encourage an open door to religious faith. The current revival of religious interest began in the colleges and universities and it has continued there. Certainly in many sophisticated circles there is today an openness to the utimate religious questions if not to traditional answers. Yet these qualifications of my earlier generalizations do not mean that what I am calling Secularist Humanism is not still the major rival of Christianity in the Western world.

I shall mention briefly two influences which give rise to this general secularist trend.

1. The first is the tendency of science with its amazing success in expanding our knowledge and our control of nature to become what is often called "scientism." This, in contrast to science, is a faith that the methods which have been so effective in the established sciences are the only significant way of knowing and that the scientific method of solving many human problems is the only way of salvation. The greatest scientists may not believe either of these things, but here I am speaking of the very widespread cultural effect of

science as the dominant element in the modern mind. This
has been said so many times that I hesitate to say it again.

It is this cultural effect of science which underlies the
idea of man's having come of age. The modern Stoics of Chapter 7 have come to realize that this faith of scientism is inadequate, that it does not really deal with the problems which
have deepest meaning for man's self-understanding and that
it offers no hope of salvation except at a very superficial level.
And yet it is probably true that the culture conditioned by
science has robbed them of the opportunity to share Christian
faith. They, as modern Stoics, are individuals who protest
against the culture, against scientism, but in wide areas of
our life the culture dominated by scientism still keeps up
appearances. There may often be a great spiritual vacuum
behind the façade even in America.

The Canadian theologian Dr. R. G. Owen, in his book *Scientism, Man and Religion,* has summarized the situation in
these words: "Modern man, because he owes so much to
science, has paid his benefactor the doubtful compliment of
transforming its working principles into universal assumptions." He then goes on to say: "It is these general assumptions, which constitute the modern pseudo-scientific
atmosphere of the age, that scientism turns into explicit and
all-embracing dogmas; science alone gives truth and this
truth is absolute; matter is primary reality; all behavior, including that of human society, is determined by impersonal
forces; all values are simply social conventions; the coming
of the ideal society is guaranteed."[3]

That is Dr. Owen's summary, but all those dogmas are
much tarnished. We live today in a period in which those
assumptions are widely questioned, though their consequences remain. The place where scientism flourishes with

fewest inhibitions is probably the Soviet Union. A good case could be made for the idea that as the everyday faith of people, scientism has greater importance in Russia than the distinctively Marxist–Leninist philosophy. Communism today, more than anything else, is scientism with emphasis upon planning by the state.

2. The second element in Secularist Humanism is the remnant of what was once a confident belief in human progress. This is related to the belief in the efficacy of science, but it also stems from a broader faith in humanity, in the moral and intellectual capacities of man. This has been the great faith of modern man especially since the eighteenth century. There was a general assumption that there is no human problem which reason and the moral will of man in history cannot solve. The appeal from any form of evil was to the future. The momentum of evolution in nature was behind the progress of man in history. This was ground common to secularism and liberal Christianity. In America the fact that a new nation was being created was a part of the stimulus for this faith. Today the fact that the Russians are creating a new civilization has much the same effect upon them. The old Christian dogmas concerning man's deep and persistent sin were renounced by many Christians and they were regarded by the secularists as evidence of the falsity and irrelevance of traditional Christian theology.

Today as we look back upon some of the illusions of our predecessors we may be inclined to exaggerate them or at least to discount the degree to which their common sense corrected many of their more foolish hopes. For example, John Dewey in *A Common Faith* protests against sentimental optimism and says that his faith in the future "makes no assumption beyond that of the need and responsibility for human endeavor, and beyond the conviction that, if human desire and endeavor were enlisted in behalf of natural ends, conditions would be bettered. It involves no expectation of a millennium of good."[4] Dewey was the great philosopher of Secularist Humanism of the first half of this century and he represented no starry-eyed utopianism but a sober meliorism. But his influence did inspire a generation of educators whose working faith was the belief in the future of problem-solving man in the framework of social and political democracy. This whole matter of progress is something which it is hard for people like ourselves to grasp. Within our lifetime we have moved from the highest expectations that men have ever held concerning their future in this world, to the darkest fears that men have ever held about their future in this world. This has happened to us, in this one life span, and it is a wonder that we are as sane as we are.

In America one of the most characteristic forms of Secularist Humanism growing out of this faith in human progress is associated with democracy. In recent years the critics of this tendency have often called it the religion of democracy. It is important to distinguish between belief in democracy as the best type of political structure, a belief which probably all of us share, and this democratic faith which is itself a substitute for religion, if not itself a religion. (Notice how throughout we must make distinctions between the secular and secularist, between science and scientism, between a reasonable hope for progress and the doctrine of progress as the meaning of human history, between democracy as a good structure and the religion of democracy.) This is both a faith in the democratic process as a method of human organization and a faith in man. One of the main historical strands in the development of democratic thought was a belief in human perfectibility. But it is important to put beside that strand the belief in democratic institutions, not because of this extreme optimism about human nature but because democracy provides for a check upon the power of sinful men. It is this less optimistic democratic faith that is embodied in the constitution of the United States and which is so well expressed in the words of Abraham Lincoln: "No man is good enough to govern another without that other's consent." Reinhold Niebuhr has stated this way of thinking in a famous epigram: "Man's capacity for justice makes democracy possible; but man's inclination toward injustice makes democracy necessary."[5] This view of democracy is itself a result of Christian insight concerning human nature. It is in no way a religious substitute for Christianity. Democracy usually becomes a religion in itself if it is combined with an uncritical view of man's possibilities when the way is cleared for the people to express themselves and to control their destiny.

There is a situation in America which often unintentionally gives encouragement to Secularist Humanism. The fact of our religious pluralism and the very desirable constitutional provision for the separation of church and state often have as an unintended by-product the encouragement of a common-denominator religious outlook which is in practice quite similar to Secularist Humanism. I believe in the American system of separation between church and state, but there are interpretations of separation which are so extreme that they discourage all positive expressions of religious faith in relation to our common life—Protestant, Catholic, or Jewish—and create a religious vacuum which is often filled in practice by a secularist type of religion which does not seem to threaten the separation of church and state.

This tendency can be seen most clearly in the field of

public education. Religious pluralism in America makes it necessary to guard against the use of the public schools by Protestants, Catholics, or Jews to teach their distinctive faiths. Americans agree concerning this in principle, though they may differ on the extent to which it is possible or appropriate to include teaching *about* the various religious traditions in the public schools in a way that is fair to all of them and which in no way seeks to indoctrinate the pupils with any one of the competing creeds. I believe that experiments should be made in this type of teaching, though I realize that it will not be easy for Roman Catholic teachers to teach objectively facts about Luther or for Protestant teachers to teach objectively facts about the Papacy. However, a discussion of this problem would take us far afield.

The main point is that there are very strong forces in America which make a virtue of emptying public education of all religious content, which oppose strenuously such experiments as "released time" weekday religious education under the auspices of the churches. Those who hold this view take an extremely negative attitude toward parochial schools in spite of the fact that parochial schools are an effort by churches to solve a real problem that is created by the understandable failure of the public schools to deal with religious issues. I realize that systems of parochial schools side by side with the public schools are divisive and that they lead to a dissipation of the educational resources of many communities. But we need to see parochial schools as an inevitable reaction to the secularization of the public schools.

This religious emptiness of public education has had two consequences which are favorable to Secularist Humanism as a fourth faith besides the three traditional faiths—Protestantism, Catholicism, Judaism. One is the simple fact that the failure of the schools, which have so much authority in the life of a child, to include religion as a significant aspect of life gives the impression that religion is marginal or dispensable. This inference may be drawn unconsciously and no one may intend to have it drawn. The other consequence is not so widespread and it may be less common now than it was two decades ago, and yet it needs some emphasis. This religious vacuum is very favorable to the inculcation of an unrecognized religion against which the formula of separation of church and state is no protection, and this unrecognized religion is likely to be the religion of Democracy or Secularist Humanism. It happens that this unrecognized religion has been very influential in educational circles. John Dewey was its prophet and he was also the most influential figure in the philosophy of education in this country for several decades.

The doctrine of the absolute separation of church and state which was promulgated by the Supreme Court in the McCollum decision in 1948 (the decision concerning the released-time scheme in Champaign, Illinois) has long been the standard around which those who seek the secularizing of American life have rallied. To some degree this decision of the court was modified by the later decision in 1952 in regard to the New York type of released-time education (the Zorach Decision). In that decision Justice William O. Douglas gave great encouragement to those who seek to find ways to counteract the secularizing tendency in public education. Two sentences especially—which to one who is not a lawyer or judge seem to represent an opposite approach from that of the Court in the McCollum decision—should be quoted: "The First Amendment, however, does not say that in every and all respects there shall be separation of Church and State."

This is quite different from the earlier talk about the "wall of separation" between Church and State. The other sentence is this: "When the state encourages religious instruction or cooperates with religious authorities by adjusting the schedule of public events to sectarian needs it follows the best of our traditions."

Now it is important to see things in perspective. There is this tendency in America, because of the religious pluralism, to encourage a common-denominator religion. But it should be said that in the nations of Europe which have state churches there is more avowed secularism than there is here. In those European countries the churches do not flourish as much as they do in America. There is no doubt that there is a remarkable revival of religious interest in America in spite of the religious vacuum in public education. This revival may be a temporary trend which will soon spend itself. But I think that today Secularist Humanism as an explicit creed is much less powerful than it was, and yet it remains the fourth American faith, and the critic of American churches from abroad is likely to suspect that Secularist Humanism in a more vague form and decked out with a combination of Christian symbols and symbols of Americanism is still far stronger than it appears to be even within the flourishing churches.

So much for a very inadequate exposition of the point of view I call Secularist Humanism. What should we as Christians say about it and in response to it?

First, it is important to realize that we are dealing here with another faith and not with science and not with an entirely neutral position which can claim to be objective. The fact that those who hold this position often claim for themselves by implication at least the authority of science confuses the issue. Also there is a tendency, especially in academic circles, to assume that a position not associated with one of the historic religious traditions is somehow more objective and more neutral religiously than Christian or Jewish or Buddhist teaching. This point has practical importance, for example, in a great state university which I have in mind, where all teaching of subject matter that can be called sectarian is excluded. All Christian or even theistic teaching is judged to be sectarian. But teaching which is dominated by Secularist Humanism is not regarded as sectarian and it can be taught by insinuation in innumerable ways in the curriculum and it can largely control the atmosphere. If you are a Christian you are believed to be biased by definition, but if you are a Secularist Humanist you are objective!

Second, there is often a great deal of misunderstanding of Christianity in the minds of those who hold this view. I do not mean that if they understood Christianity they would necessarily accept it, but often their rejection is premature because they associate Christianity with some kind of Fundamentalism. They assume that Christian teachings belong to an outmoded world-view, that they involve acceptance of the dogma of the infallible Bible, that they involve many particular formulations of doctrine which today are often rejected by Christians themselves. Often they assume that Christianity is associated with a loveless legalism, with an essential lack of charity toward all who are not "righteous" or toward all who do not accept particular doctrines. If the truth about the Christian gospel were known, it would often surprise the critics at this point. For the Christian gospel is the proclamation of the love of God for all men, and its judgment falls hardest on the self-righteous and the loveless who delight in excluding others from the circle of the redeemed.

There is an especially difficult problem in the rejection of Christian faith by those who identify it with a narrow individualism or an otherworldly spiritualism which is indifferent to the inhumanity and injustice of social systems. Communists as well as many Secularist Humanists assume that the churches stand for social reaction because during the rise of modern capitalistic industrialism, they were identified with the privileged classes and were blind to the injustices of early capitalism. In the past three generations the churches, both Catholic and Protestant, have waked up to their responsibilities in this area to some extent, but there is a record to be lived down.

Third, we could point to many inadequacies in Secularist Humanism as a faith. It has gained its strength because of an earlier optimism about human progress and about the sufficiency of science which today can be seen to be untenable. The Christian conception of man is far more realistic than the usual Secularist Humanist conception of man. It makes room not only for the greatness of man, for his high possibilities, but also for the deep roots of human evil, for the tragic contradictions in man's nature. Indeed, it is my expectation that the most thoughtful Secularist Humanists will find themselves pushed into something like the Stoicism described by Dr. Driver in Chapter 7 unless they are drawn to a more positive faith, such as the Christian faith. It is difficult to remain a very confident Secularist Humanist when you live on the edge of a nuclear catastrophe which if it came would be a consequence of a tragic mixture of science with political conflicts and ideological confusions.

Fourth, our central answer to Secularist Humanism is an affirmation of faith, just as Secularist Humanism is itself fundamentally an affirmation of faith.

It is an affirmation that there is an ultimate meaning in human life and in human history that cannot be contained in the secularist position. This ultimate meaning for us involves the conviction that our experience depends upon a creative divine mind and purpose which transcend nature and history. Often this affirmation has been put in terms of proofs or arguments for God, but these have failed to convince those who did not begin with this basic faith—theistic faith, if you want a name for it. I am not sure that this level of affirmation would at the end of the day convince even me if there were not the other and more specifically Christian level of affirmation.

We affirm that God is a transcendent creator who has not left the world to itself, for we believe that there is a series of events in which God has acted decisively to reveal himself to us and to redeem us. These events begin with the first responses of the people of Israel to the call of God; they become more convincing in the responses of prophets and psalmists; at the center of these events is the coming of God to his people in Christ, in his life and teaching, in his death and resurrection. All of this might be only past history for us if we did not also believe that in Christ there came into the world a new order of life, new beginnings, new possibilities. Theologians describe this new order in a great variety of ways, and some of them identify it with the visible Christian community or church. I should be more reserved than that and say that the church is the institution and community which can relate us to this new order, that the church witnesses to the new order when it is true to itself, but the church always is a human institution and community which remains under the judgment as well as under the Lordship of Christ. But these refinements would take us very far from our subject. My main point is that the Christian answer to Secularist Humanism is not an argument or another religious philosophy. It is the affirmation that the God whose reality may be affirmed as the source of the ultimate meaning of our life "has visited and redeemed his people," has come to us centrally in Christ. We affirm not an idea but a new reality in our history and in our life today. This is a whole new way of looking at the world, which we can learn only from response to the data of the biblical revelation. The Old Testament revelation has within itself great power to convince and does not depend wholly upon the New Testament for its significance, but we do see it fulfilled in a wonderful way in the New Testament. The rejection of this faith often comes from a failure to attend to it, a failure to listen to what it really is. This is often because Christians in their lives misrepresent it. It calls for decision, but not decision in the dark, for Christians believe that, in spite of all the difficulties which it does raise, when once one starts with it as the clue to existence, large areas of our life are illumined.

I am concluding this chapter by giving one specific example of how the Christian faith does illumine a certain aspect of our life where the Secularist Humanist has the greatest stake, and that is the relationship of our faith to democratic values. I am not suggesting that some particular democratic institutions are necessary; I am not using Christianity as a prop for American democracy; but there are democratic values which are valid and which the Secularist Humanist has greatly stressed and there are aspects of Christian faith by which these values are supported.

There are at least three factors in the Christian faith (more broadly in the biblical faith) which are favorable to these democratic values. Democratic ideas may come from many

sources, not least from Greek philosophy and constitution-
making, but I am referring not to ideas as much as to com-
mitments and habits of feeling without which the ideas do not
long remain embodied in the life of a community. These three
factors are: (1) The recognition that every human power
stands under the judgment and the mercy of God so that
men find themselves saying, "We must obey God rather than
men." This is the surest source of personal freedom, of the
limited state. (2) The confidence that God cares for the
dignity and the welfare of all persons regardless of status,
that he seeks especially to defend those who do not have
the power to defend themselves, the poor who have been sold
for a pair of shoes, the anonymous victims who have fallen
among thieves. (3) The confession on the part of worshiping
men that they are sinners, that they must look first to their
own sin rather than to the sin of their neighbors or opponents,
that each must consider the beam in his own eye rather than
the mote in his brother's eye.

These elements in biblical religion need to be kept in
balance. Any one of them can be distorted, especially when
emphasized apart from the others. Let me give you some
examples of these distortions. When a particular religious
group or church claims a monopoly of understanding of the
will of the transcendent God or when a nation or party claims
that God is wholly on its side, this very faith in God's transcendent judgment is distorted and it becomes an instrument
of tyranny and fanaticism. No one in church or state has
seen this more clearly than Abraham Lincoln, who confessed
that God's will transcended even his own cause in the great
conflict of his life. He found, when he said this, "that men
are not flattered by being shown that there has been a difference of purpose between the Almighty and them." Indeed

they are not, especially when their opponents happen to be atheists, as is the case with America today. In Christian history there has been a continual conflict between the conservative use of the idea of divine providence as the support for the status quo and the revolutionary implications of the divine love for the weak and the exploited.

The respectable groups which have held social and political power, when they have also been the guardians of religious truth, have often applied their doctrine of sin to the masses of humanity more than to themselves. (That was true of the Federalist clergy in New England when they thought about the "rabble" that followed Jefferson and Jackson in the early days of the Republic.) Often they have feared anarchy on this account more than they have cared for justice. But within the sphere of the church even the righteous and the respectable and the powerful can be brought to realize that they too share the common sin of humanity, that their power needs to be governed by law, that it should even be checked by the power of those who are affected by their decisions. I realize that this last concession on the part of men of power may often be no more than an acceptance of a *fait accompli*. Sometimes one generation fights these checks upon power and the subsequent generation accepts them. There is an element of grace in this process by which these restraints and checks are accepted. I think that history has helped Reinhold Niebuhr to make his point that democracy depends both upon hope in the common man and upon an understanding of the universality and persistence of sin. Political conflict is the generator of massive self-righteousness where there is no understanding of the sin of man on both sides of a conflict. It is always difficult to admit that we do not have a monopoly of truth and virtue, but even a slight concession on this point may make possible the balancing of power and the compromises of interest, the grace of mutual respect and the beginnings of charity without which there can be no realization of democratic values.

I recognize that religious self-righteousness can be the most destructive kind and that when it is combined with political self-righteousness, hell can break loose. This is one point at which the secularist has often had a salutary role to play, though since there is no God above his cause, he is in danger of making his cause into God and his self-righteousness may even exceed that of the religious man who claims the support of God for his cause. The biblical religions have within them correctives for this perversion. It is the great tragedy of Communism that its atheism and its identification of evil by definition with the economic system of its adversaries rob it of these correctives. I must say here that just as the secular is important for us to recognize, so too, it is true that the secularists have frequently been very necessary critics of the churches and of religious people.

There is an ancient story of a king and a prophet which points to the source of some of the values we cherish. To illustrate the king's own crime against Uriah, the Prophet Nathan told King David the parable of the rich man who stole the poor man's lamb (II Sam., ch. 12). When David became indignant against the villain in the parable, Nathan closed in on him and said, "Thou art the man." This story illustrates the fact that even the king who had the political power recognized that he was under God and that there were limits to what he could do to his subjects, that Uriah and the poor man had rights which the king and the rich man were obliged to respect. Here we have the limited state; here we have the rights of all men as men. Some things we must add to these—such as regular channels by which the citizens can protect themselves against the king and also protection against the prophets when they forget that they are not God. But here is indeed a great treasure which we have inherited and which we take too much for granted.

Many believe that the justice and the charity and the freedom which are embodied in American institutions can continue without reference to the traditional faith. It is obvious that they are right so far as individuals are concerned and perhaps even so far as generations are concerned. I must record my own skepticism as to whether self-spending compassion for the least of men, who have no claim, will continue as a powerful social force if there should pass out of the dim awareness of men that we are all, from the least unto the greatest, objects of the divine love. I also question whether loyalty to the community will be strong without absolutizing the community and the will of those who have most power in it, if it is forgotten that the community is not a law unto itself, that it lives under God's righteousness and mercy. I do not suggest that there can be no embodiment of democratic values unless a nation has a strong Christian tradition—but I do suggest that these values, which are the chief concern of Secularist Humanism, point beyond themselves to a deeper source of meaning and raise problems which Secularist Humanism cannot solve.

7. Christianity and Stoic Existentialism

TOM F. DRIVER

Those philosophies and movements that today would supplant Christianity take many forms, according to the aspects of Christianity that each would replace. Communism feeds on Christian social ideals. Certain kinds of psychiatry aspire to take over Christianity's cure of souls. In the spiritual realm, the major rival to Christianity adopts what Professor Roger Shinn has called "the existentialist posture."

Existentialism as such is not a rival to Christian faith. On the contrary, without its own existential component Christianity would become mere theory. Yet there is a strong tendency within existentialist thought—where that thought turns in upon itself—that moves directly counter to Christian faith. We shall try to identify that tendency and to show how it constitutes the major alternative alive today for persons religious in temperament but who do not believe that Christianity is any longer a genuine option.

I

Existentialism is a transitory philosophy. As an "ism" with exponents and adherents, it is a phase of thought moving between two much more stable and creative points of view. Existentialism is born in Romanticism and grows toward Stoicism.

Romanticism began in the late eighteenth century as a vigorous, almost volcanic, eruption of elements in man that had been submerged by three centuries of confident humanism, faith in reason, and faith in universal harmony. The emotional component in man revolted.

Not that the Romantic movement was all emotion and no thought. Far from it. Astute and great minds hammered out its ideas with no little labor. The object, nonetheless, was a way of reasserting the value of man's emotional life in a world that had more and more come to be understood as rational, systematic, and subject to explanation by scientific means. Romanticism was a protest against the separation of subjective man from the objective world, a separation that the age of Reason had perhaps unwittingly brought about.

Romanticism was also a reaction against the false optimisms of eighteenth-century politics. It was the experience of the French Revolution and its aftermath that made a Romantic out of Wordsworth. In the beginning he had seen the revolution as many liberal optimists of his time saw it— something to clear out the debris that stood in the way of men's reasonable hopes and rights. The aftermath, the tyranny and the ruthlessness of Robespierre, shattered Wordsworth, forcing him to reconstruct his understanding of human nature and history. It taught him that human decisions, human sympathies, and human emotions are the all-important part of the equation. Wordsworth thereafter devoted himself to the exploration of the heart of man in its relation to the external world. A similar line of thought had already begun in Germany with such thinkers as Fichte, Novalis, Schelling, and the brothers Schlegel.

If we see Romanticism as a reaction against the objectivity and false optimism of the age of Reason, we understand many of its features. From this reaction arises its nostalgic (and often unrealistic) love of ages and civilizations long passed as well as its love of nature, especially nature wild and uncultivated. The Romantics loved ruins of Gothic cathedrals and Roman and Greek temples. In ruins, nature is reclaiming to her own domain the temporary artifacts of man, while history is judging man's rational–liberal pretensions. Even the liberalism of Shelley did not preclude his Romantic fascination with the desert's victory over Ozymandias.

The drive within Romanticism to be reunited with nature explains why one of the master images of Romanticism is that of the bodily *organism*. A. W. von Schlegel was using the true Romantic vocabulary when, in his "Lectures on Dramatic Art and Literature," delivered in 1809, he said that dramatic form is bad when it is mechanical but good when it is organic. Within the body, of course, the "vital" organ is the heart, and so it went hand in hand with the other aspects of Romanticism that it should search for truth via the heart, that is, through the emotions. For man was to be organically related to his world, not merely intellectually related. The basic question Romanticism asked was how man could belong to his world. In a sense we are still in the Romantic period, for we have not quit asking that question. Indeed, the question becomes more acute as the march of science goes steadily forward, leaving behind a cloud of human anxiety about what it means to be man in a heedlessly objective world. Sometimes the Romantics, in their urge to belong, fled to other worlds—to the past, or to the ideal, or, as we shall see later, into the arms of death itself. But the steadier among them stood firm and asked over and over again how man might belong to the natural world in which he lives. Wordsworth represents the kind of "firm Romanticism" from which Existentialism was born.

Many of Kierkegaard's mentors were of the Romantic school. In literature there was Novalis, in whom the romantic love of night and death was so strong. In philosophy, there was Schelling. Like the Romantics, Kierkegaard was in reaction against ways of thought that by-passed human will and emotion. He lashed out at Hegel's "system" in the name of the desires, the will, and the decisive importance of the unique individual, for whom matters of life and death could never be decided by any structure of rational thought, however objectively "true" it might seem to be. The trouble with Hegel's system, according to Kierkegaard, was that it *was* a system, that it pretended from an objective standpoint to take account of everything, that it rationalized the entire process of history in such a way that man's inwardness, his irrational subjectivity, was not taken into account.

The contemporary philosophers who have taken their lead from Kierkegaard—Heidegger, Sartre, Marcel, Jaspers—continue the reaction against depersonalizing tendencies in science, technology, and politics. They are the modern bearers of the Romantic protest, which they have deepened and worked out in philosophical terms. Likewise, our Existentialist literature is a continuation of the Romantic literature of the last century.

Modern Existentialism is Romanticism that has been put

through the fires of twentieth-century brutality and philosophical Positivism. We may well ask what happens to Romanticism when it is asked to suffer in the way that modern man has known suffering. He has experienced great physical suffering caused by the political chaos of our age and also suffering of a mental or psychological form caused by the interior collapse of meaning and values. Though it is part of the Romantic make-up that it likes to flirt with pain, the pains of the modern world have been relentless enough to force even Romanticism to shift its ground. It has moved toward Stoicism.

II

Three principal elements in existentialist Romanticism engender Stoicism. These are its individualism, its sense of brotherhood, and its attitude toward death.

Ancient Stoicism arose in a period when world politics seemed nearly as chaotic as they do in our day. The glory of Athens had passed. The conquests of Alexander the Great had recently been made, but already there was discord among his successors. The age of Roman imperialism had not yet arrived. The world was very sophisticated, but also very weary. Stoicism, like its rival philosophy Epicureanism, was a means of giving dignity and purpose to the individual, who might otherwise be lost in irrelevant philosophical speculation or destroyed by the capricious turnings of history. As Moses Hadas has put it, "Men turned from first philosophies and speculations on the ideal state, which they could never conceivably do anything to make real, to systems which would help them endure life in a terrifying large world which reduced them to ciphers."[1] Through the rest of the Classical period Stoicism cultivated self-reliance, so that nothing in the external world would be able to shatter the poise and worth of the individual.

Epictetus reports the story of Priscus Helvidius, a Stoic he admires. This man refused an order of the emperor Vespasian, for which Vespasian threatened to put him to death. Priscus Helvidius replied: "You will do your part, and I will do mine: it is your part to kill; it is mine to die, but not in fear: yours to banish me; mine to depart without sorrow."[2]

To be sure, ancient Stoicism gave courage to the individual by appealing to what it called Reason, which governed the world through Natural Law. Nothing corresponding to such a principle is found in our contemporary Existentialism. Stoic "Reason," however, was not something purely objective to which the individual had merely to conform. On the contrary, "Reason" was what belonged to the true nature of the individual. "In order to determine the rational and the irrational," said Epictetus, "we use not only the estimates of external things, but we consider also what is appropriate to each person."[3] Such language is easily translatable into the terms of an Existential philosophy like that of Heidegger. Heidegger's "unauthentic existence" is life determined according to "the estimates of external things"—that is, from without—making the individual conform to a pattern, either intellectual or social. "Authentic existence" is living according to "what is appropriate to each person," as Epictetus would say—that is, according to the unique requirements of the self as these come to be recognized and assumed *by* the self. Sartre holds that the individual literally makes himself into himself by making decisions. This is the ethic of Stoic self-reliance pushed to the ultimate degree and supported by a new philosophy.

In the thought of Jaspers, Sartre, and Heidegger, individualism is combined with an emphasis upon responsibility for one's fellow human beings. The seeds of this attitude were already present in Romanticism. At its best, Romanticism encouraged sympathy and compassion for all creatures. As it longed for a more perfect union between man and nature, so it yearned for identification between man and man. This is very clear in Wordsworth; for instance, in his poem "The Solitary Reaper":

> Behold her, single in the field,
> Yon solitary highland lass!
> Reaping and singing by herself;
> Stop here, or gently pass!
> Alone she cuts and binds the grain,
> And sings a melancholy strain;
> O listen! for the vale profound
> Is overflowing with the sound.

Romantic empathy, here so delicately expressed by Wordsworth, is one of the springs from which flows that sympathy for the downtrodden, the outcast, the criminal, the prostitute and the like which floods modern fiction. Existentialism carries this sympathy further than Romanticism, combines it with the sense of individual responsibility already mentioned, and arrives at an advocacy of human brotherhood. One sees this best in Camus.

Camus himself performed the Stoic act he so often counseled in his writing: he took the burdens of others upon his own shoulders. As Francois Mauriac said when Camus died, "A whole generation became aware of itself and of its problems through Camus. . . . And it is all youth that mourns him at this moment." Camus' pre-eminent position did not

come to him by accident. It came because he asked for it—
not to win glory for himself, but simply because it was necessary that someone should labor to make his generation "aware
of itself and its problems." He forged a link between himself
and the men of his times. He undertook to examine their fears,
their sense of futility, their responsibilities, their guilt, their
necessity to rebel against tyranny. He became the man who
experienced their inner life for them and brought it to light
in his prose.

One of Camus' best stories is called *The Growing Stone*.
It is about a Frenchman who finds himself in a small Brazil-
ian village on the eve of a local celebration called the Feast
of the Good Jesus. D'Arrast, the Frenchman, meets a man
who has been a ship's cook and who is now living among the
impoverished natives of the village. Some time ago, the cook
had been cast into the sea when his ship caught fire and sank
off the coast near this place. While struggling in rough waters
he looked to shore and saw light from the church of "the
good Jesus." He told "the good Jesus" that at his procession
he would carry a hundred-pound stone on his head if he,
Jesus, would save him. Thereupon the waters became calm
and the man swam slowly and happily to shore. Now it is the
eve of the procession, and the cook tells D'Arrast of his
promise. They take part in the native dancing, which goes on
with savage fury through the night. The next morning the
cook begins his march with the stone. But he is too weak
from the night's reveling to finish. Exhausted, he lets the
stone fall to the ground, his body pouring sweat, tears coming
from his eyes. Without a word D'Arrast pushes the crowd
aside and lifts the stone. He begins to walk toward the church.
The cook's rash promise is absurd. D'Arrast has no faith in
"the good Jesus" and sees no reason why, if there were a good

Jesus, he should desire the cook to carry a stone on his head. Yet the task is there, and D'Arrast decides to finish it. With the stone on his head, he walks. He does not, however, go all the way to the church. In a decision as quick and unmeasured as his first one, he swerves from the path and goes toward the river. Then, turning again he goes to the hut that belongs to the cook. There at last he hurls the stone into the fireplace amid the ashes. Then he leans against the wall of the hut with his eyes closed. Soon the hut's inhabitants come in, the cook as well, and they gaze at the stone, the stone they had expected to see at the altar of the shrine but which they now see at the hearth instead. They sit down around it.

Standing in the darkness, D'Arrast listened without seeing anything, and the sound of the waters filled him with a tumultuous happiness. With eyes closed, he joyfully acclaimed his own strength; he acclaimed, once again, a fresh beginning in life. . . . The brother moved a little away from the cook and, half turning toward D'Arrast but without looking at him, pointed to the empty place and said: "Sit down with us."[4]

In this story are combined most of the elements that go to make up the Existentialist form of Stoicism: individualist self-reliance; the absurdity of human labors, since they lead to nothing; and yet the value of identifying with one's brother, whoever he may be, and of sharing with him the laborious absurdity that goes to make up living. The cook makes his decision alone. D'Arrast makes his decision alone. But they end sitting together beside the hearth.

The third element in existentialist Romanticism that feeds modern Stoicism is its attitude toward death.

In his book *Love in the Western World,* Denis de Rougemont has traced the Romantic attitude toward love, passion, and death through the history and literature of Europe since the twelfth century. It began among the poets and troubadours of southern France who glorified passion. The Lady whom they constantly addressed in poem and song was none other than Night or Death, to which they looked for the ultimate fulfillment and negation of desire. This cult of night and knighthood took on mythical expression in the story of Tristan and Isolde, which has become the central myth of adultery, passion, and fulfillment-in-death for Western man. De Rougemont finds the root of the Romantic passionate ideal in the heretical Catharist movement that flourished in southern France also during the twelfth century and can be traced ultimately to the Manichaean doctrines of Persia; the created world is regarded as evil and man's deliverance comes when death takes him out of the world and into the realm of the eternal.

The Romantic is always a yearner after a pristine purity, a lost harmony that he cannot find in present experience. Eventually his yearning turns to death itself as the ultimate object of his desire. Death is the ultimate ecstasy.

No one who knows Wagner's opera *Tristan und Isolde* will be in doubt as to what is meant. Wagner's music fuses the desire for death and the desire for passion. Its climax is the *Liebestod*.

Eugene O'Neill affords a recent example of this type of Romanticism. In *Long Day's Journey into Night*, Edmund Tyrone describes one of his few happy moments in life, a time when he lay aboard a ship at sea and looked up at the sky:

Dreaming, not keeping lookout, feeling alone, and above, and apart, watching the dawn creep like a painted dream over the sky and sea which slept together. Then the moment of ecstatic freedom came. The peace, the end of the quest, the last harbor, the joy of belonging to a fulfillment beyond men's lousy, pitiful, greedy fears and hopes and dreams! And several other times in my life, when I was swimming far out, or lying alone on a beach, I have had the same experience. Became the sun, the hot sand, green seaweed anchored to a rock, swaying in the tide. Like a saint's vision of beatitude. Like the veil of things as they seem drawn back by an unseen hand. For a second you see—and seeing the secret, are the secret. For a second there is meaning! Then the hand lets the veil fall and you are alone, lost in the fog again, and you stumble on toward nowhere, for no good reason! . . . I will always be a stranger who never feels at home, who does not really want and is not really wanted, who can never belong, who must always be a little in love with death![5]

Existentialism gives the Romantic attitude to death a decidedly Stoic turn. Death becomes the inescapable fate with which one has to live. In O'Neill's play *The Iceman Cometh*, the Romantic and the Stoic attitudes are both present. Hickey, the iceman, propels himself and his friends into death's arms while Larry Slade, the detached philosopher of the play, becomes "a convert to death"—that is, one who will not try to escape his fate but will henceforth live with death as his companion.

Seneca, the Roman Stoic, spoke of a *libido moriendi,* a desire for death, a term very close to Freud's "death instinct."[6] For the Stoic, death is not only inescapable, it is always there as a possible means of asserting one's superiority over the necessities and vicissitudes of life. Epictetus referred to death as an "open door." "Remember this," he said, "the door is open. . . . When things seem to you of such a kind, say I will no longer play, and be gone; but if you stay, do not complain."[7] Similarly Sartre has suggested that suicide may be a means to contract out of an existence into which one has been thrust not of his own will. The hero of Camus' novel *The Stranger* declares as he is about to be executed: "How could I fail to see that nothing was more important than execution . . . and that it was even, in a way, the only really interesting thing for a man?"

III

That there are differences between modern and ancient Stoicism is only too clear. The early Stoicism, we remember, was grounded in a philosophical principle of universal law and reason. The universe was not absurd, it was ordered and predictable. Immortality was certain. And we recall that great sense of detachment from the world which Tillich calls Stoic "superiority and complacency." In all these respects ancient Stoicism was very different from the modern.

Nevertheless, the similarities between the old and new Stoicisms may seem to us even more impressive:

1. Both are means of overcoming human anxiety about death and fate. They face it squarely without trying to say that it does not exist. Even with their belief in immortality the ancient Stoics did not think that death was an illusion or that it was not a threat.

2. Both demand courage as the primary ethical virtue. Tillich has highlighted this in his book *The Courage to Be,* a work which owes much to the new Stoicism, even though it is grounded in Christian faith.

3. Both demand as the second most important human virtue the attitude of resignation. One is asked to be resigned to his fate, whatever that may be. True, the Existentialist be-

lieves that man partly makes his own fate through his decisions, but he can do this only after he has become resigned to the ultimate futility and absurdity of human endeavor.

4. Both require that one remain faithful to his individual self in all matters pertaining to ethics. That is, both propose a radically nonconformist ethic because both place highest value upon conformity to the self. They therefore require and cultivate the virtue of self-reliance.

5. Both maintain a positive or at least a potentially positive attitude toward the act of suicide.

6. Both emphasize that all men are part of a single, world-wide community.

In short, modern Stoicism addresses many of the same problems as did ancient Stoicism and it cultivates a similar ethic in response to them. It does not, of course, arrive at its position through anything like the philosophy of ancient Stoicism, but like its predecessor it asks man to live with courage and resignation.

IV

If we look for manifestations of Stoicism in the modern world, we find that our literature is full of it. I have already mentioned Camus, Sartre, and Eugene O'Neill. Consider also these lines from Robert Frost:

> I have been one acquainted with the night.
> I have walked out in rain—and back in rain.
> I have outwalked the furthest city light.
>
> I have looked down the saddest city lane.
> I have passed by the watchman on his beat
> And dropped my eyes, unwilling to explain.
>
> I have stood still and stopped the sound of feet

> When far away an interrupted cry
> Came over houses from another street,
>
> But not to call me back or say good-bye;
> And further still at an unearthly height,
> One luminary clock against the sky
>
> Proclaimed the time was neither wrong nor right.
> I have been one acquainted with the night.[8]

The Stoic note resounds in Faulkner's assurance that man, amid corruption, will "endure," and he did not change it very much when he said that man will "prevail."

Stoicism dominates the work of Tennessee Williams. There one clearly sees the Romantic and Existentialist elements combine and then move ever closer to Stoic courage. In *Camino Real*, Williams extolled Romantic courage, the courage of risk, which took the dare and ventured across the desert void that most men fear to contemplate. In *Sweet Bird of Youth*, Chance Wayne teases the powers that can destroy him, and in the end he does not flee those who come to mutilate him. Williams writes: "He wasn't driven out of the town he was born in." In other words, he develops the Stoic courage of resignation.

A similar kind of power sustains Anton Schill, the protagonist of Friedrich Dürrenmatt's play *The Visit*. This man also refuses to be driven from his native town, even though the people have turned against him and will take his life, acting upon a perverted sense of justice. His mood is very like that of Priscus Helvidius, whom Epictetus cited: "It is your part to kill; it is mine to die, but not in fear." Schill says in the play: "Now I have conquered my fear. Alone. It was hard, but it's done. And now you will have to judge me. And I will accept your judgment. For me that will be justice. How it will be for you, I don't know."[9]

We find here and there a quieter kind of Stoicism also. For instance, in the poetry of Wallace Stevens. Stevens is *par excellence* the poet who celebrates the secular world of "things as they are" and of things as they are transformed by the human imagination. Both the objective world and the imagination of man, however, exist for Stevens independent of Divine Creation. "We live," he writes

> in an old chaos of the sun,
> Or old dependency of day and night,
> Or island solitude, unsponsored, free.

The beauty of "Sunday Morning," surely one of the most moving poems ever written by an American, is evidence enough of the attraction of the Stoic attitude among us. Earlier in the poem Stevens speaks of death:

> Death is the mother of beauty; hence from her,
> Alone, shall come fulfillment to our dreams
> And our desires. Although she strews the leaves
> Of sure obliteration on our paths, . . .
> She makes the willow shiver in the sun. . . .
> Is there no change of death in paradise?
> Does ripe fruit never fall, . . .
> Death is the mother of beauty, mystical,
> Within whose burning bosom we devise
> Our earthly mothers waiting, sleeplessly.

The Romantic sigh for the absolute peace of death here reaches us in the sweetest of whispers. Stevens does not rush forth to find the absolute. Rather, he absorbs it into his experience of nature and thought. The serenity thus achieved accounts for the note of infinite resignation upon which the poem ends:

Deer walk upon our mountains, and the quail
Whistle about us their spontaneous cries;
Sweet berries ripen in the wilderness;
And, in the isolation of the sky,
At evening, casual flocks of pigeons make
Ambiguous undulations as they sink,
Downward to darkness, on extended wings.[10]

V

If Stoicism can present itself as a rival to Christianity this
is precisely because the two have so much in common. It is
easy to cite quotations from Christian literature that sound
as if they had been written by Stoics, and vice versa. Tertul-
lian referred to Seneca as "our Seneca," and well he might,
for that Stoic sage had not only ideas but also words and
phrases that were very close to many in the New Testament.

What, then, are the points of similarity between Christianity and Stoicism, and what are the differences? We shall be
content with four similarities and then one all-important
difference.

1. Stoicism and Christianity unite in asserting the importance of the individual over against the depersonalizing forces
of society and science. The Stoic is a dissenter, and the
Christian also is, or should be, a dissenter. In this regard,
modern Christianity has much to learn from Stoicism, for
most of the great dissenters in our day, those who have had
the courage to say No, have been Stoics.

2. Stoicism and Christianity both acknowledge, even while
they speak of individualism, that there is a community unit-
ing men. Thus, the dissent of both the Stoic and the Christian
comes from the fact that they put themselves into *commu-*

nities of dissent. If they stand against the world, they do so because they know they belong to a genuine community the world has not yet acknowledged. For the Stoic, this genuine community may be the community of reason, as it was with the ancients. It may be the community of a new movement or political state, as with many Marxists and other revolutionaries who have what Tillich calls Stoic participation. For the Christian, the genuine community is that of the church and the company of apostles, saints, and martyrs who are in the church invisible. Potentially, for both the Stoic and the Christian, the genuine brotherhood includes all men, though all men do not yet acknowledge it.

3. Building upon self-reliance and participation in the community, both Stoicism and Christianity call for courage. Both the Stoic and the Christian are called to take up arms in the battle of life. Paul admonishes Timothy to fight the good fight, and Seneca writes to Lucilius that "life is warfare."[11] Sartre admonishes the Stoic Existentialist to become *engaged* in the struggles of the world, and the title of this book speaks of "Christianity on the March."

4. Both Stoicism and Christianity require that the self be "given over" to something outside itself. For the Christian, this means to the divine will and pleasure, while for the Stoic it means fate or destiny. In their outward appearance these attitudes are so similar that it is often hard to distinguish them. In the famous speech in the fifth act of *Hamlet*, for instance, the Stoic and Christian elements are so mixed that commentators have never agreed which is predominant. Says Hamlet:

We defy augury. There's a special providence in the fall of a sparrow. If it be now, 'tis not to come; if it be not to come, it will be now; if it be not now, yet it will come; the readiness is all. Since no man has aught of what he leaves, what is't to leave betimes? Let be.[12]

It is perhaps impossible to tell whether this is a giving over of the self to the will of divine providence, being ready for whatever He shall appoint, or whether it is mere Stoic fatalism.

If Stoicism and Christianity hold much in common, there is yet one aspect in which they differ entirely, and that one is sufficient to outweigh all the similarities. Where Stoicism cultivates an attitude of *cosmic resignation*, Christianity believes in *cosmic salvation*.[13] For Stoicism, the world as it exists cannot be changed. Nothing within it or outside it works for its re-creation. With the ancient Stoics, this was because the world was already ruled by external reason. With the modern Stoics, though man may make himself over by his actions and decisions, this has nothing to do with bringing the world into harmony with its intended destiny. As far as the world is concerned, one leaves it in a state of resignation.

Christianity, on the other hand, lives or dies in the belief that God is reconciling to himself a world that has been divorced from him. Christians believe, therefore, in *cosmic salvation*, and this belief is particularly important at the present moment in history.

VI

Many signs tell us that we are emerging from the period of Existentialism. The public, by and large, has lost its fascination with the Existentialist mode of thought. Existentialism places one at the edge of a great abyss, and people will, if they can, move away from such a precarious location at the first opportunity.

In moving from Existentialism, which way shall we go? The *natural* tendency is to go toward Stoicism, for Existentialism is born in Romanticism, passes over the abyss of Nothingness, and tends to grow into Stoic resignation.

Like Romanticism, Christianity knows a longing. It knows the desire of man, who is estranged from his Creator, to be reconciled to him. Christianity knows also the abyss that Existentialism knows. It feels the abyss of despair that opens when one sees his estrangement from God and his infinite guilt before God. But Christianity knows something that secular Existentialism does not know: namely, that above the abyss, or beneath the abyss, as we may choose to say it, there is a God of Creation who reaches forth with his hand, and with his suffering self, to close the gulf that separates man and God. The Christian believes that God will make creation new. Death is not the final word. Resignation is not the final moral act. The final word is resurrection. The final moral act is faith in the sovereignty of the Redeeming God.

The choice between the moral act of resignation and the moral act of faith is the choice that faces most persons today. For a time it may seem that the choice is between faith and materialism. Americans may entertain themselves with all those recreations that *Life* magazine calls ironically the Good Life. Persons in other parts of the world may be busy for some years establishing new governments, aiding the industrial revolution in their countries, and bringing themselves "up" with the rest of the world. But it will not be long in this age of rapid change before all discover what the Hellenistic world discovered: that to put one's faith in the natural world and in empirical knowledge about it is in the long run simply to rush toward despair, because the natural world is sooner or later destroyed, as Aristotle said, in the clang of the teeth of time.

Whenever a man or a society comes of age—Western European society *has* come of age and America is close behind— it knows that the fundamental choice is between the moral act of resignation and the moral act of faith. Of the two, the moral act of resignation, though hard, is yet the easier, for it lies entirely within one's own control. The moral act of faith, on the other hand, is something one cannot perform unless God in his own way shall produce faith within him. So the choice is not, accurately, between resignation and faith but between resignation and expectation of faith. The words are Prospero's:

> And my ending is despair
> Unless I be relieved by prayer.[14]

This is the situation in which the Christian gospel must be preached today. The comfort of prosperity is only a diversion. The issue is death or life.

Notes

PART I: CHRISTIANITY'S MARCH THROUGH HISTORY

1. The Beginning: Turning the World Upside Down

1. *Mar. Pol.* 8.
2. *Trypho* 2.
3. *Confessions* 8.2.
4. *Protreptikos* 12.
5. Aristides, *Apology* 15.

3. Confronting the Modern World: The Last 150 Years

1. "The Missionary Implications of the End of Western Colonialism and the Collapse of Western Civilization," *History's Lessons for Tomorrow's Mission: Milestones in the History of Missionary Thinking* (Geneva: World Student Christian Federation, n. d.), p. 200.
2. *Our Country: Its Possible Future and Its Present Crisis* (New York: Baker & Taylor Co., 1885), pp. 3 f.
3. George Hodges, *Faith and Social Service* (New York: Thomas Whittaker, 1896), p. 61.
4. Richard M. Fagley, "The Population Explosion," *Social Action*, XXV (Dec., 1958), 5 f.
5. Bert J. Loewenberg, "Darwinism Comes to America," *Mississippi Valley Historical Review*, XXVIII (1941), 361.

6. *The Crisis in the University* (London: S. C. M. Press, 1949), p. 138.
7. D. T. Niles, "The Present Situation and Prospect," in Stephen Neill (ed.), *Twentieth Century Christianity* (London: Collins, 1961), p. 421.
8. From a sermon preached by Edward D. Griffin at Sandwich, Mass., Oct. 20, 1813, quoted by Oliver W. Elsbree, *The Rise of the Missionary Spirit in America*, 1790-1815 (Williamsport, Pa.: Williamsport Printing, 1928), p. 130.
9. "Christian Ethics," in Arnold S. Nash (ed.), *Protestant Thought in the Twentieth Century: Whence and Whither?* (New York: The Macmillan Company, 1951), p. 138.
10. *Religion and the Modern World* (New York: Frederick A. Stokes Co., 1929), pp. 26 f.
11. *Religion in Our Times* (New York: Round Table Press, 1932), p. 156.
12. *The Twentieth Century in Europe: The Roman Catholic, Protestant, and Eastern Churches* (New York: Harper & Row, 1961), p. 539.
13. *History's Lessons for Tomorrow's Mission*, p. 199.
14. *The Age of Reform: From Bryan to F. D. R.* (New York: Alfred A. Knopf, 1956), p. 326.
15. On the latter point, and for the American scene, cf. Will Herberg, *Protestant—Catholic—Jew: An Essay in American Religious Sociology* (Garden City, N.Y.: Doubleday & Co., 1955), and Peter L. Berger, *The Noise of Solemn Assemblies: Christian Commitment and the Religious Establishment in America* (Garden City, N.Y.: Doubleday & Co., 1961).
16. *The Twentieth Century in Europe*, pp. 539 f.
17. *A Catholic Primer on the Ecumenical Movement* (Westminster, Md.: Newman Press, 1957), p. ix.
18. *One Great Ground of Hope: Christian Missions and Christian Unity* (Philadelphia: Westminster Press, 1961), p. 15.
19. Niebuhr, in collaboration with Daniel Day Williams and James F. Gustafson, *The Purpose of the Church and Its Ministry: Reflections on the Aims of Theological Education* (New York: Harper & Row, 1956), pp. 16 f.
20. *Preaching and the New Reformation* (New York: Harper & Row, 1956), p. 10.
21. *A Theology of the Laity* (Philadelphia: Westminster Press, 1958), pp. 91 f.

22. For a good introduction to this, see Massey H. Shepherd (ed.), *The Liturgical Renewal of the Church* (New York: Oxford University Press, 1960).

23. "The Church of Rome" in Neill (ed.), *Twentieth Century Christianity*, p. 49.

24. *Ibid.*, pp. 33-81.

25. Cf., e.g., Robert McAfee Brown and Gustave Weigel, *An American Dialogue: A Protestant Looks at Catholicism and a Catholic Looks at Protestantism* (Garden City, N.Y.: Doubleday & Co., 1960), and Daniel J. Callahan, Heiko A. Oberman, and Daniel J. O'Hanlon, S.J. (eds.), *Christianity Divided: Protestant and Roman Catholic Theological Issues* (New York: Sheed and Ward, 1961).

26. W. H. T. Carter, *Echoes from Edinburgh, 1910: An Account and Interpretation of the World Missionary Conference* (New York: Fleming H. Revell Co., n. d.), pp. 56 f.

27. Franklin H. Littell, *The German Phoenix: Men and Movements in the Church in Germany* (Garden City, N.Y.: Doubleday & Co., 1960), p. 186.

28. *One Great Ground of Hope*, p. 11.

PART II: CHRISTIANITY TODAY

4. Christianity Today: An Eye-Witness Report

1. Robert S. Bilheimer. *What Must the Church Do?* (New York: Harper & Row, 1947), p. 80.

2. *One Great Ground of Hope: Christian Missions and Christian Unity* (Philadelphia: Westminster Press, 1961), p. 15.

3. Bernard Leeming, S.J., *The Churches and the Church* (Westminster, Md.: Newman Press, 1960), p. vii.

4. George H. T. Kimble, *Tropical Africa* (2 vols.; New York: Twentieth Century Fund, 1960), II, 202-9. Paperback ed. (New York: Doubleday & Co., Anchor Book, 1962), II, 218-25.

5. Adapted from Henry P. Van Dusen, *For the Healing of the Nations* (New York: Charles Scribner's Sons, 1940), pp. 17-24.

6. *One Great Ground of Hope*, pp. 133-34.

PART III: CHRISTIANITY AND ITS MAJOR CONTEMPORARY RIVALS

6. Christianity and Secularist Humanism

1. New York: The Macmillan Company, 1954; p. 146.

2. New York: Philosophical Library, 1949; pp. 161-62.
3. New York: Philosophical Library, 1949; p. 55.
4. New Haven: Yale University Press, 1934; p. 46.
5. *Children of Light and Children of Darkness* (New York: Charles Scribner's Sons, 1944), p. xi.

7. Christianity and Stoic Existentialism

1. Hellenistic Culture: Fusion and Diffusion (New York: Columbia University Press, 1959), p. 23.
2. *Discourses* I. ii.
3. *Ibid.*
4. *The Exile and the Kingdom* (New York: Alfred A. Knopf, 1958), pp. 212-13.
5. New Haven: Yale University Press, 1956; pp. 153-54.
6. See Paul Tillich, *The Courage to Be* (New Haven: Yale University Press, 1952), p. 11.
7. *Discourses* I. xxiv.
8. "Acquainted with the Night," from *Complete Poems of Robert Frost.* Copyright 1928 by Holt, Rinehart and Winston, Inc. Copyright renewed (c) 1956 by Robert Frost. (New York: Halcyon House, 1939), p. 324. Reprinted by permission of Holt, Rinehart and Winston, Inc.
9. *The Visit,* adapted by Maurice Valency (New York: Random House, 1958), p. 101.
10. From *Collected Poems* (New York: Alfred A. Knopf, 1955), p. 66. Reprinted by permission of the publisher.
11. *Epistles* 96:3.
12. Shakespeare, *Hamlet,* Act V, Scene 2, lines 230-35
13. I am indebted to Paul Tillich for the italicized phrases. *Op. cit.,* p. 15.
14. Shakespeare, *The Tempest,* Epilogue.

Bibliography

1. The Beginning: Turning the World Upside Down

BAMM, PETER. *The Kingdoms of Christ* (From the Days of the Apostles to the Middle Ages). New York: McGraw-Hill Book Co., Inc., 1962.

HARNACK, A. *The Mission and Expansion of Christianity.* New York: Harper Torchbooks, 1961.

LATOURETTE, KENNETH SCOTT. *The First Five Centuries.* New York: Harper & Row, 1937.

LIETZMANN, H. *The Beginnings of the Christian Church.* New York: Charles Scribner's Sons, 1937.

——. *The Founding of the Church Universal.* New York: Charles Scribner's Sons, 1938.

PETRY, RAY C. *A History of Christianity,* Vol. I. Englewood Cliffs, N.J.: Prentice-Hall, Inc., 1962.

RICHARDSON, C. C. *The Church through the Centuries.* New York: Charles Scribner's Sons, 1938.

VAN DER MEER, F., AND MOHRMANN, C. *Atlas of the Early Christian World.* New York: Thomas Nelson & Sons, 1958.

WALKER, W. *A History of the Christian Church.* New York: Charles Scribner's Sons, 1959.

(173)

MAKERS OF XTY: S. J. CASE
J. McNEILE
W. W. SWEET

2. The Great Crisis: The Reformation of the Sixteenth Century

BAINTON, ROLAND H. *Here I Stand.* The Life of Martin Luther. Nashville: Abingdon Press, 1950.
——. *The Reformation of the Sixteenth Century.* Boston: Beacon Press, 1952.
BOEHMER, HEINRICH. *Road to Reformation.* Philadelphia: Muhlenberg Press, 1946.
HUIZINGA, JOHAN. *The Waning of the Middle Ages.* London: E. Arnold & Co., 1924.
PAUCK, WILHELM. *The Heritage of the Reformation.* Glencoe, Ill.: Free Press, Second Edition, 1961.
RUPP, E. G. *Luther's Progress to the Diet of Worms.* Chicago: Wilcox & Follett, 1951.

3. Confronting the Modern World: The Last 150 Years

GAUSTAD, EDWIN S. *Historical Atlas of Religion in America.* New York: Harper & Row, 1962.
HUDSON, WINTHROP S. *American Protestantism.* Chicago: University of Chicago Press, 1961.
LATOURETTE, KENNETH SCOTT. *Christianity in a Revolutionary Age.* 5 vols. New York: Harper & Row, 1958-1962.
NEILL, STEPHEN C., ed. *Twentieth Century Christianity: A Survey of Modern Religious Trends by Leading Churchmen.* London: William Collins Sons & Co., 1961.
NICHOLS, JAMES H. *History of Christianity, 1650-1950, Secularization of the West.* New York: Ronald Press & Co., 1956.
SMITH, H. SHELTON, HANDY, ROBERT T., AND LOETSCHER, LEFFERTS A. *American Christianity: An Historical Interpretation with Representative Documents.* 2 vols. New York: Charles Scribner's Sons, 1960-1963.
SMITH, JAMES W., AND JAMISON, A. LELAND. *Religion in American Life.* 4 vols. Princeton: Princeton University Press, 1961- .

4. Christianity Today: An Eye-Witness Report

CAVERT, SAMUEL McCREA. *On the Road to Christian Unity.* New York: Harper & Row, 1961.

GOODALL, NORMAN. *The Ecumenical Movement: What It Is, and What It Does.* New York: Oxford University Press, 1961.

HOGG, W. RICHEY. *One World, One Mission.* New York: Friendship Press, 1960.

NEWBIGIN, J. E. LESSLIE. *The Reunion of the Church.* New York: Harper & Row, 1948.

———. *A Faith for This One World?* New York: Harper & Row, 1961.

VAN DUSEN, HENRY P. *World Christianity: Yesterday, Today and Tomorrow.* Nashville: Abingdon Press, 1947.

———. *One Great Ground of Hope: Christian Missions and Christian Unity.* Philadelphia: Westminster Press, 1961.

VISSER 'T HOOFT, W. A. *The Pressure of Our Common Calling.* Garden City, N.Y.: Doubleday & Co., Inc., 1959.

5. Christianity and Its Major Rivals in Asia

ALLEN, E. L. *Christianity among the Religions.* London: George Allen and Unwin, 1960.

APPLETON, GEORGE. *On the Eightfold Path: Christian Presence Amid Buddhism.* London: S.C.M. Press, 1961.

COOKE, GERALD. *As Christians Face Rival Religions.* New York: Association Press, 1962.

CRAIG, KENNETH. *Call of the Minaret.* New York: Oxford University Press, 1959.

———. *Sandals at the Mosque.* New York: Oxford University Press, 1959.

HAMMER, RAYMOND. *Japan's Religious Ferment: Christian Presence Amid Faiths, Old and New.* London: S.C.M. Press, 1961.

KRAEMER, H. *The Christian Message in a Non-Christian World.* London: Lutterworth Press, 1939.

———. *Religion and the Christian Faith.* London: Lutterworth Press, 1956.

———. *Why Christianity of All Religions?* London: Lutterworth Press, 1962.

6. Christianity and Secularist Humanism

BENNETT, JOHN C. *Christians and the State.* New York: Charles Scribner's Sons, 1958.

BONHOEFFER, DIETRICH. *Prisoner for God.* New York: The Macmillan Company, 1953.

DEWEY, JOHN. *A Common Faith.* New Haven: Yale University Press, 1934.

FARMER, H. H. *Toward Belief in God*. New York: The Macmillan Company, 1943.

FRANKEL, CHARLES. *The Case for Modern Man*. New York: Harper & Row, 1956.

FROMM, ERICH. *Marx's Concept of Man*. New York: Frederick Ungar Publishing Co., 1961.

HERBERG, WILL. *Protestant-Catholic-Jew*. Garden City, N.Y.: Doubleday & Co., 1956.

JENKINS, DANIEL. *Believing in God*. Philadelphia: Westminster Press, 1956.

LAMONT, CORLISS. *Humanism As a Philosophy*. New York: Philosophical Library, Inc., 1949.

NIEBUHR, H. RICHARD. *Radical Monotheism and Western Culture*. New York: Harper & Row, 1960.

NIEBUHR, REINHOLD. *Self and the Dramas of History*. New York: Charles Scribner's Sons, 1955.

OWEN, D.R.G. *Scientism, Man, and Religion*. Philadelphia: Westminster Press, 1952.

RUSSELL, BERTRAND. *A Free Man's Worship*. Portland, Me.: T. B. Mosher, 1927.

TILLICH, PAUL. *The Dynamics of Faith*. New York: Harper Torchbooks, 1958.

7. Christianity and Stoic Existentialism

CAMUS, ALBERT. *The Myth of Sisyphus*. New York: Alfred A. Knopf, 1955.

——. *The Exile and the Kingdom*. New York: Alfred A. Knopf, 1958.

HERBERG, WILL. *Four Existentialist Theologians*. Garden City, N.Y.: Doubleday & Co., 1958.

ROUGEMENT, DENIS DE. *Love in the Western World*. New York: Harcourt, Brace and World, Inc., 1940.

SARTRE, JEAN PAUL. *Existentialism and Humanism*. London: Methuen & Co., Ltd., 1955.

SHINN, ROGER L. *The Existentialist Posture*. New York: Association Press, 1959.

TILLICH, PAUL. *The Courage to Be*. New Haven: Yale University Press, 1952.

Format by Sidney Feinberg
Set in Linotype Caledonia
Composed, printed and bound by American Book–Stratford Press, Inc.
HARPER & ROW, PUBLISHERS, INCORPORATED

DATE DUE